Governing Trade Unions in Sweden

Governing
Trade Unions
in Sweden

LEIF LEWIN

Harvard University Press

Cambridge, Massachusetts, and London, England · 1980

331.8809485
L67g

Library of Congress Cataloging in Publication Data

Lewin, Leif, 1941–
    Governing trade unions in Sweden.

    Translation of Hur styrs facket?
    Bibliography: p.
    Includes index.
    1. Trade-unions—Sweden. I. Title.
HD6757.L4813   331.88′09485   79-26724
ISBN 0-674-35875-9

Preface

This inquiry into trade union democracy is closely related to earlier research, including my own study *Folket och eliterna* [*The People and the Elites*]. That book scrutinized postwar political science theory on the subject of democracy and led to my formulation of the model of interactive democracy. Every study of democratic processes requires some organized concept of the principles of democracy. Interactive democracy provides one of many possible frameworks for a systematic analysis. After my publication of the democratic model, I looked around for material whereby it could be tested.

In formulating a model, a series of hypotheses is set forth, based on the findings of generally accepted research. These hypotheses concern the internal relationships of certain phenomena and processes in democratic organizations. But such relationships can be verified only through individual tests conducted in accordance with certain principles. *Governing Trade Unions in Sweden* subjects the model of interactive democracy to precisely such a test.

This inquiry also derives from a presentation of the process of political science research that I gave in my inaugural lecture entitled "Statskunskapen, ideologierna och den politiska verkligheten" ["Political Science, Ideologies, and Political Reality"]. There I argued that, contrary to what is usually done, an attempt should be made to combine theory based on the history of ideas with empirical testing. The outline of that lecture has been followed in this book, which is divided into five chapters—each corresponding to one of the five steps enumerated there. First, a model is constructed based on the normative theory found within the problem area—a model that can then serve as the basis for testing; chapter 1 takes up the question of how democratic organizations should be governed, leading up to a presentation of the model of interactive democracy. Second, this model is specified in order to make it relevant to the particular problem area under study; chapter 2 deals with the specific governance problems of the Swedish trade union movement. Third, the researcher engages in empirical observations of the reality he wishes to study; chapter 3 discusses fieldwork and findings. Fourth, the actual testing correlates empirical observations with the original model; chapter 4 classifies and explains the various forms of union government. Fifth, conclusions are drawn; chapter 5 returns to the initial normative problem and shows how this study of the problems of democracy within the Swedish trade union movement has provided deeper insight into the model of interactive democracy.

A number of persons have contributed to this research project. First, my thanks go to the Bank of Sweden Tercentenary Fund, whose financial support made the study possible. Trade union officials—in the various locals, in the secretariats of the national unions, and in the central office of the Swedish Federation of Trade Unions—have been most helpful in providing the necessary information.

My closest associate has been Barbro Lewin, who patiently checked each individual step and was responsible for the fieldwork as well as the coding. She was assisted periodically by several helpers. Bo Jansson, whose wealth of ideas is a stimulating asset to any research project, was mainly responsible for the sampling. Dag Sörbom processed the data at Uppsala Datacentral with his customary speed and efficiency. Many students contributed, through research papers and in other ways; foremost among them are four students pursuing independent research programs that fall within the framework of this volume: Erik Åsard, Ingemar Backman, Axel Hadenius, and Sven-Erik Svärd. Special gratitude is extended to Sverker Gustavsson, Axel Hadenius, and Olof Petersson for their important comments on the manuscript, and to the many trade union and committee members at various levels, who through their responses to the questionnaire made this study possible. Finally, my warm thanks go to Kjersti Board for her careful rendition of this study into English.

L. L.

Contents

Tables

Figures

Governing Trade Unions in Sweden

1

How Should Democratic Organizations Be Governed?

Is the Swedish trade union movement governed by "bosses," unrepresentative of the general membership? Or is the union movement on the whole characterized by a smoothly functioning democracy? These questions have again been raised during the 1970s. The first few years of the decade witnessed an intense debate in the mass media concerning the problems of union democracy. Behind this debate lay the criticism by the international New Left of the political establishment—in Sweden identified as the leaders of Landsorganisationen [LO, Swedish Trade Union Confederation]—coupled with the new unrest on the Swedish labor market, which was symbolized by the widespread miners' strikes of 1969 and 1970. Besides these main questions a number of special problems were included in the debate. What is the extent of the support among the rank and file for LO's policy of wage solidarity? Does the new wave of wildcat strikes represent a protest against a policy of equalization of wages which has been carried too far? What has been the effect on union democracy of the consolidation of locals into district branches? How do union elections function? What is the role played by the collective affiliation of trade union locals with the Social Democratic Party? To what extent do the leaders dominate the members? Does an oligarchy exist within the Swedish labor movement today and can oligarchy be avoided? Is an efficient central bureaucracy needed to defend the interests of the rank and file?

As a theoretical background to the empirical study of these problems, this chapter will discuss how leading political philosophers and scientists have confronted the problem of governance of democratic organizations and relate their formulations to developments in Sweden.

Michels and Oligarchy within the Workers' Movement

In the early 1900s, a young German was traveling around his country for the purpose of studying the Social Democratic Party, at that time the largest socialist party in the world and the model for many workers' parties around the globe. His name was Robert Michels, by profession a social scientist, by political persuasion a socialist. The more he studied the German workers' movement, the more critical he became of the internal conditions of the party and the labor unions. For within these organizations, which through their advocacy of general suffrage and democracy led the fight against the bureaucracy and elitism of the antidemocratic Empire, Michels discovered a far-reaching centralization of power in the hands of a few. In 1911 he published his thoughts on oligarchy within the workers' movement in a study entitled *Zur Soziologie des Parteiwesens in der modernen Demokratie* (1911). This study has become a classic in the field of social science. Many, to their surprise and disappointment, have been forced to agree, sometimes with a sigh of resignation or with a cynical smile, with his description of the dominating position of the leaders at the expense of the general membership. This is still the case today. In light of the present tendencies of concentration within the labor union movement, an ever increasing number of observers agree with Michels that there no longer exists—and possibly never did exist—anything resembling trade union democracy.

According to Michels, the bureaucratization of the workers' movement could not be attributed to the ill will, lust for power, or corruption of the leadership. The rise of an oligarchy was inevitable. Modern democracy inexorably tended toward replacing political equality with leaders and the led, and Michels perceived this development as a law, formulated in the English edition of his work as "the iron law of oligarchy." Criticism of labor leaders for a lack of radicalism in union policy missed the point. Oligarchy was caused not by ideology but by organization. The domination of the electors by the elected was based on organization: "Who says organization, says oligarchy."[1]

It was a scientific triumph for Michels to be able to prove that the iron law of oligarchy applied also to the socialist workers' movement. To demonstrate the existence of an oligarchy within the conservative parties would have been pointless because they did not regard themselves as democratic. But to show that not even the party that championed the introduction of democracy had escaped the inexorable drift toward oligarchy made Michels's book a powerful polemic. According to Michels, modern oligarchy within the labor organizations began when Karl Marx exhorted the proletarians of the world to unite. Michels still regarded the proletariat as the weakest class in society. In order to raise their living standard, the workers would have to organize. The fight against the proponents of capitalism required well-disciplined, socialist fighting organizations. With just a few words, Michels dismissed the unrealistic dream that organization might not be necessary or that direct popular participation or legislation might be effective methods in the struggle between the classes. On the contrary, he said, the workers' movement needed efficient leaders, well trained in the newly emerging party schools, leaders who received authorization for their plans of attack from the members and who had a sure grasp of the strengths of the movement. The oligarchic camarilla that developed in this way contrasted sharply with the ignorance and indifference of the masses vis-à-vis union politics. But the leaders themselves underwent a curious psychological transformation during the process of organization. Officials from the most proletarian backgrounds began to feel like the new masters when, instead of holding jobs that required physical labor, they were placed in positions that required them to demonstrate intellectual superiority and financial resourcefulness and to engage in negotiations and administration. They adopted the refined mannerisms of the bourgeoisie, often affecting a kind of pseudoculture and arrogance. In Michels's view, a truly representative leadership was impossible. The need for an organized labor movement had inevitably created union managements that, with their technical skills and efficiency, no longer mirrored the wishes and interests of the masses. The main concern of the leadership was no longer the realization of socialism, but the maintenance of the gigantic union and political party apparatus.

Michels criticized the workers' movement only with difficulty. Basing his conclusions on exhaustive and laborious investigations, he delivered his admonitions without betraying his loyalty toward the party with whose program he sympathized. For he was convinced that, in the long run, this kind of outspokenness would benefit the party. It was the task of social science to contribute to the education of the citizens so that they would be more inclined toward critical and controlled action and thus, as far as possible, be able to counteract the oligarchic tendencies within the labor movement. "Democracy is a treasure which no one will ever discover by deliberate search. But in continuing our search, in laboring indefatigably to discover the undiscoverable, we shall perform a work which will have fertile results in the democratic sense . . . Nothing but a serene and frank examination of the oligarchical dangers of democracy will enable us to minimize these dangers, even though they can never be entirely avoided."[2] Only three years after the publication of his book an event occurred that forcefully convinced many observers that Michels's analysis of the bureaucratic conservatism within the workers' movement was correct. Within the Socialist International, the German Social Democratic Party had acted as the foremost proponent of world peace, had implacably opposed the war policy of the Empire, and had threatened a general strike in the event of war. However, in 1914 the party immediately supported the German declaration of war. Disappointed in the Social Democratic Party, Michels wrote a bitter postscript to his book in which he discussed the party in time of war. He never doubted that the party's support of the war policy was caused by the modern oligarchy within parties and organizations. "The party gives way, hastily sells its international soul, and, impelled by the instinct of self-preservation, undergoes transformation into a patriotic party. The world-war of 1914 has afforded the most effective confirmation of what the author wrote in the first edition of this book concerning the future of the socialist parties."[3]

Empirical and Normative Theory

Is the development of oligarchic tendencies within labor organizations really an iron law? Michels presented no remedy and recommended no norms of action, although he formulated the problem more clearly than anyone before him. Michels's dilemma can be formulated thus: the introduction of democracy demands such undemocratic means of fighting, including vesting leaders with excessive power and authority, that the goal is lost through the building of the tactical organization. This seemingly insoluble paradox has dominated the debate on the organizational problems of the labor movement ever since. Even today, the political debate concerning trade union democracy finds nourishment in Michels's observation that there exists within labor organizations a tendency toward oligarchy, or "bossism." In this study, Michels's dilemma constitutes a challenge as well as a point of departure.

Michels tells of threatening dangers, but indicates no sure way of escaping them. Although Michels's work may be interpreted in many different ways, it is first an example of empirical theory, a study of how something actually is—an observation based on factual experience. In the tradition of empirical research pioneered by Michels, many questions have been asked: Was Michels right? Are there oligarchic tendencies within the modern party and organizational systems? Is oligarchy universal? Then, within the context of this tradition, the main question of this book is: Does an oligarchy exist within the Swedish labor union movement of today?

Shortly after the publication of Michels's work, political theoreticians began to propose measures designed to counteract oligarchic tendencies. Thus arose a substantial normative theory—how something should be—

concerning the governance of democratic organizations. An interesting and complex relationship exists between empirical theory and normative theory. Even the researcher in the empirical tradition is forced into normative postulates during the preliminary definition of terms necessary for subsequent analysis. For by selecting one definition of, for example, "representative leadership" over another, he also indirectly states his opinion of how democratic organizations should be governed. However, it has to be stressed that normative theory in political science does not allow individual subjective judgments about good or bad objectives for the system. A political scientist does not necessarily personally approve of the place to which his application of normative theory within his research area leads him; what the individual researcher thinks privately is of no concern. A certain critic may not approve of the normative model that a research team has established for its investigation, but this does not prevent him from determining for himself the extent to which the system accomplishes what the team intended. It is quite possible to determine empirically whether a certain society or organization is governed by a specific form of rule, regardless of the researcher's bias. For once having defined "representative leadership" and thereby having made a normative value judgment, it is possible to study whether a certain organization does or does not show evidence of such leadership, without worrying further about value judgments or political desiderata. From a normative point of view, the question raised in this book is: How should democratic organizations, such as the Swedish labor union movement, be governed in order to avoid rule by oligarchy? The question will be answered by a selective historical review of political theory, by the adoption of a general model for democracy, and by its adaptation to the governance problems of the Swedish trade union movement.

Thus, both the normative aspect of this inquiry—how democratic organizations ought to be governed and how the danger of oligarchy ought to be avoided—and the empirical aspect—to what extent the Swedish labor union movement has managed to escape that danger—are to be viewed against the background of Michels's dilemma.

Rousseau and Direct Democracy

Jean Jacques Rousseau in *Contrat social* (1762)[4] advocated a direct democracy of the people. It would replace a form of government reserved for an exclusive social and political elite. He envisioned a political body in which people would discuss matters without any leader and would harmoniously arrive at common decisions. In advancing the concept of

the general will and will of all, Rousseau rejected the idea of ruling
bodies and representative leadership within democratic organizations.
For "sovereignty cannot be represented," and to delegate power to a
leader was a crime against the "general will." According to Rousseau, oligarchy is avoided within democratic organizations by not appointing or
electing any ruling body at all.

Rousseau's terminology and ideology were adopted by radical critics
of the Social Democratic Party in Sweden, who, in 1917, broke with the
party to form the Left Socialist Party. A new, more democratically organized party would replace the bureaucratized party apparatus, which
C. N. Carleson had described in *Makt och parti i modern organisation*
[Power and Party in Modern Organization]: "Our period does not yet
belong to democracy, but to oligarchy, disguised as democracy, and
based on the discipline of the masses."[5] The oligarchy was particularly
manifest within the Swedish workers' movement, especially in the labor
unions. "In no area of the workers' movement has centralization reached
such a state of uniform perfection as in the activities of the unions, which
actually ought to be described as lacking in activity. Even more striking
than the ossification of the party is its bureaucratization, where the originally vital solidarity in the fight against capitalist exploitation gradually
has hardened to the passivity of an immovable discipline. The union official, reelected year after year, is now as all-powerful within his organization as the director of a company within his domain. As for the trade
union congresses, they have begun to resemble board meetings where
trustees and officials bargain with representatives of the shareholders."[6]
In several places, Carleson returned to how ruthlessly the union leadership had taken advantage of the notion of solidarity in order to achieve a
centralization of power.

The opening speech at the founding congress of the Left Socialist
Party emphasized the importance of learning from the experience of the
old party. It was considered necessary to protect the party against a development "in the same direction, toward rule by bureaucracy, leadership, and officials,"[7] and the new party's so-called democratic
constitution sought to express such guarantees. Leaders could not be dis-
pensed with altogether, although it was clear that the speaker at the congress had this Rousseauist norm of action in mind. Carleson wrote: "To a
certain extent, representation goes against the idea of popular sovereignty."[8] A set of rules was established to prevent the rise of an oligarchy. The democratic constitution thus states that the party has no need
for a chairman; that the members of the working committee may not
serve for more than two consecutive years; that the party paper would

devote space to opposing views; that members of the executive committee must not try to impose their will through threats of resignation or
other ultimata; that a question should be decided by referendum if a
certain number of members so request; that a special program committee should make certain that the party platform be kept sacred, a duty
that also included reporting any leader or official who was found "dan-
gerously wanting in democratic spirit."[9]

In this way a very loose party organization was established, built according to horizontal rather than vertical principles. After its formation
several labor unions collectively left the Social Democratic Party, and a
new union organization, Svenska Fackoppositionen [Swedish Union Op-
position], was created.

Would these new workers' organizations, steeped in direct democratic
idealism, prove effective in the struggle against the employers, who more
and more concentrated their own resources in the hardening fight over
wages? Outside the ranks of the Left Socialists themselves there were
few who believed in that possibility, and within a few years this experiment was dead. The Swedish Union Opposition never attracted enough
members and was dissolved, and the party underwent a dramatic shift toward centralism. The attempt to follow, as far as possible, the Rousseauist action norm had failed. There are very few records of other
equally serious attempts of this kind in the history of the European workers' movement.

The failure of this experiment does not mean that Rousseau's norm of
action has proved irrelevant to the formation of political theory. By
steadfastly maintaining the principle of political equality within democratic organizations, even when it interferes with the ability of an organization to work for its program with undiminished vigor, Rousseau's
action norm seems unusually consistent and straightforward.

Weber and the Efficiency of Bureaucracy

Max Weber was Michels's teacher. His influence on the scientific development of his pupil cannot be overestimated.

Weber's fields of research were vast and widely divergent.[10] Along
with Marx he must be regarded as the most influential social scientist of
the time. Weber's studies on the efficiency of bureaucracy greatly influenced Michels's research on the governance problems of the labor
unions. According to Weber, when the leadership attempted to persuade
the rank and file of the legitimacy of its exercise of power it could appeal
to three different types of authority. The first is "charismatic" authority,

based on an extraordinary affection held by the membership for a leader
with unusual, saintly, or heroic qualifications, such as religious leaders,
political demagogues, or military heroes. The second type of authority is
"traditional," founded on inherited customs, often affording the will of
the leader a considerable degree of leeway—the traditional monarch
being the typical example. The third form of authority is "legal," in
which the area of jurisdiction for different officeholders is carefully regu-
lated by generally valid laws. The foremost example of this last form of
authority is modern bureaucracy. Weber regarded bureaucracy as the
most rational form of organization and believed that because of its
greater efficiency it would render obsolete all traditional or feudal forms
of rule in the same way that machines had rendered obsolete nonme-
chanical means of production in an industrialized society. In the area of
party politics, Weber maintained with Michels that a strong party apparatus was a prerequisite for victory. He was painfully aware of the tendency for conflict between efficient leadership and broadly based,
popular political participation. As Sverker Gustavsson states: "Especially
the section on modern party politics gives rise to the odd mixture of fas-
cination and discomfort which seems to characterize our present-day impression of Weber. He forces the reader to consider how the constant
rationalization and bureaucratization in this era of mass democracy gradually is changing government by the people into a race in which elite
groups vie for the favor of the masses."[11]

Objections have been raised to Weber's analysis of rule by bureaucracy. Empirically, is bureaucracy really as efficient as Weber claimed?
For bureaucracy is often labeled as slow, awkward, and inefficient. Furthermore, an organization that meets all of Weber's criteria for an efficient bureaucracy cannot be maximally rational, because of con-
tradictions in those criteria. From the normative point of view, it is more
important to note that Weber was so interested in the efficiency of gov-
ernmental forms that he lost sight of their democratic aspects. He never
subjected the idea of democracy to systematic analysis. He viewed democracy as a form of legal authority, although he made it clear that legal
rule was not always democratic; bureaucracy, not democracy, became
the prototype for legal order. Bureaucracy achieves the highest degree of
efficiency; therefore, Weber perceived it as the most rational tool for
controlling the people. Indeed, Weber's appreciation of the efficiency of
bureaucracy was so great that his language "vibrates with something of
the Prussian enthusiasm for the military type of organization."[12]

According to Peter M. Blau, Weber should have made a distinction
between organizations that are formed for members who want to work

on a common program of action, and those that exist for the pursuit of goals that are already agreed on. The former organization is democratic, the latter bureaucratic. However, such a distinction cannot always be maintained, because an organization can serve both purposes. "The distinction is an analytical one, since many organizations have the dual purpose of first deciding on collective goals and then carrying out these decisions. As a result, the two principles come into conflict. Unions are a typical example. Democratic freedom of dissent and majority rule are often set aside in the interests of administrative efficiency and effective accomplishment of union objectives."[13]

In the attempt to scrutinize some norms for the governing of democratic organizations and to follow the above thought to its logical conclusion, one could ask whether it is really necessary that labor unions be democratically organized. Workers join unions because of a commonality of interests, namely, higher wages, shorter work hours, better working conditions, and so forth, which the unions have to realize as effectively as possible. Then, is it not possible that bureaucratically or even militarily organized unions would be more effective in the struggle against the employers than those democratically organized? The British trade union specialist V. L. Allen, who was greatly influenced by Weber, maintained that the most rational form of government for the unions is the one "to which Max Weber refers, at the expense of 'self-government.' "[14] Allen viewed the development of a bureaucracy within the union movement as indicative of the tendency of democracies to seek authoritarian solutions to important problems. He formulated an action norm for the organization of trade unions: "In other words, the end of trade-union activity is to protect and improve the general living standards of its members and not to provide workers with an exercise in self-government."[15]

The view that political-democratic models cannot automatically be applied to unions and that an efficient central bureaucracy is needed to defend the interests of the rank and file, which is the goal of the union movement, has found great support in recent debate on union democracy in Sweden. These arguments have often been used by labor union leaders against critics inspired by the theories of Rousseau. An editorial, "Centralism or Not? Striking Power the Most Important," in *Fackföreningsrörelsen* [Trade Union Movement], the official organ of LO, argued:

> The workers' movement—LO and the Social Democrats—has often been accused of pursuing a policy of centralism, and of possessing a top-heavy organizational structure . . . The LO part of the Swedish union movement is [however] neither centralistic nor decentralistic. Neither centralism nor decentralism is of any value in and of itself. The important thing is

which forms of organization and decision, within the framework of democracy, can best serve the interests of the membership . . . What some
groups today refer to with disdain as the LO bureaucracy consists of people with expertise to offer the elected representatives of the employees'
associations. There are economists capable of meeting the economists of
Capital, doctors capable of meeting the doctors of Capital, lawyers capable of meeting the lawyers of Capital, and journalists capable of meeting
the journalists of Capital. This central power apparatus is needed to meet
the central power apparatus of Capital, in the same way as the local rank
and file is indispensable for the local struggle.[16]

The action norm emerging from labor union research inspired by
Weber, with strong support also in the Swedish union debate of today, is
thus almost the exact opposite of Rousseau's recommendation. According to the latter, it is necessary to be prepared to sacrifice effectiveness
for political equality; according to the norm that is being defined here,
the correct procedure consists of choosing the form of organization that
most effectively serves the common interests of the membership. This
means that the democratic form of organization is rejected in favor of an
efficiently developed bureaucracy. Without a strong position for the governing board and the experts, the trade union movement would be incapable of pursuing its goals with any hope of success. It cannot be denied
that this recommendation is every bit as clear and consistent as Rousseau's norm of action.[17]

Lenin and the Revolutionary Vanguard

Lenin, too, realized that the workers' movement needed strong leaders.
He spent the first two decades of this century traveling from one European city to another, ceaselessly agitating for a new direction for the socialist strategy; he especially criticized the German Social Democratic
Party for its reformism and lack of theoretical insight. As had Michels
before him, Lenin spoke of the ignorance and inertia of the masses and,
as did Weber, recommended centralization of power in order to achieve
the greatest possible success. But, in contrast to Weber, he did not oc-
cupy himself primarily with the general aspect of the problem of authority. Lenin scrutinized the demands which the socialist revolution
would place on leadership and organization. In his view, the leaders of
the workers must constitute the revolutionary vanguard, preparing to
seize power and spurring the workers on to action. Lenin spoke dis-
paragingly of socialists who thought that the collapse of the capitalist
system, which was predicted by Marx, would occur spontaneously, ac-

cording to some predetermined laws of economic development, without hard work by the party. The proletariat could be freed from the shackles of capitalism only through armed struggle. To assure victory it was necessary to understand what Marxism meant in the contemporary historical context as well as for the organizational development of the workers' movement. "Concrete analyses of concrete situations" had to be made. Lenin proved to possess an unusual ability to apply the philosophy of Marx and Engels. His party theory has become famous for its significance, effectiveness, and ruthlessness. When the power of the czar began to falter, Lenin returned to Russia, and a surprised world witnessed his theories as they were put into practice in the creation of modern Soviet society.

According to Lenin, one of the most serious defects of the workers' movement was that it was trade unionist in nature: it defended the material interests of its members by union methods—negotiations and conflicts with the employers. The lot of the working class would not be improved substantially within the framework of the capitalist system. Capitalism had to be crushed. The world proletariat had to take over the means of production. Therefore, work within the political party had to take precedence over work in the trade unions, and all forces had to be directed toward preparing the workers for the revolution. The organizational principle that had to be used in this process is referred to as "democratic centralism." It consists of an almost total concentration of power in the hands of an inner circle. Lenin and his followers justified their calling this form of government democratic by pointing to the purpose behind the organization—to free the people from capitalism. Without the existence of an elite party the workers would not be mobilized for the uprising. For, as Lenin clearly indicated, the workers had no spontaneous revolutionary consciousness. The Party was to be small, secret, and composed of dedicated professional revolutionaries. Alongside the Party there were to be large, open labor organizations for the mobilization of the broad mass of workers. At the critical moment these union organizations were to be subordinated to the "general staff" of the working class, the Party. In a revolutionary situation, distinguished by a sudden intensification of a number of tensions and conflicts in society, the workers, under the leadership of the Party, would seize power and crush the bourgeois apparatus of the state. A dictatorship of the proletariat would be established, during which violence and terror would be directed against the fallen bourgeoisie, until this class had been obliterated. Then the apparatus of the state, which had always been an instrument of violence for the ruling class, but had been, during the dictatorship of the

proletariat, an instrument of violence directed against lingering bourgeois elements, would disappear. The Party would exercise control and
oversee all phases of production. Gradually, the people would become
accustomed to this accounting and control. "Armed workers" would
learn to supervise the former capitalists, now civil servants, and watch
for tendencies toward "capitalist backsliding"; in other words, the workers themselves would learn to lead, and the hold of the Party would begin
to slacken.

> For when all have learned to manage, and independently are actually
> managing by themselves social production, keeping accounts, controlling
> the idlers, the gentlefolk, the swindlers and similar "guardians of capi-
> talist traditions," the escape from this national accounting and control
> will inevitably become so increasingly difficult, such a rare exception, and
> will probably be accompanied by such swift and severe punishment (for
> the armed workers are men of practical life, not sentimental intellectuals,
> and they will scarcely allow any one to trifle with them), that very soon
> the *necessity* of observing the simple, fundamental rules of everyday so-
> cial life in common will have become a *habit*.
>
> The door will then be wide open for the transition from the first phase
> of Communist society to its higher phase, and along with it to the com-
> plete withering away of the state.[18]

Considering how many people are influenced by it in their daily lives,
Lenin's party theory is probably the most successful in history, and the
Swedish Left Socialists, mentioned previously, were most receptive to it.
Influenced by Michels's criticism concerning oligarchy within the workers' organizations, these idealists had adopted a far-reaching, direct-dem-
ocratic principle of organization inspired by Rousseau. They now did an
about-face and made their party extremely centralistic. Immediately
after World War I, communist parties sprang up in Europe, inspired by
Lenin's revolution in Russia and the faltering European monarchies and
empires. Many socialists considered a revolution imminent also in Sweden. A considerable number of Swedish Left Socialists began to turn toward Lenin's party theory. In 1921 the Comintern adopted the so-called
Twenty-one Theses, a concentrated expression of Lenin's strategy. When
the Swedish party tried to adopt them, a fight naturally ensued. For the
Twenty-one Theses were in flagrant opposition to the so-called democratic constitution that had been adopted only three years earlier. For
pacifist or tactical reasons, many speakers also disassociated themselves
from violence and terror, and they rejected the idea of an armed working
class. But Leninism emerged victorious; as a result, a faction left the
party. The following year the Leninist direction was confirmed when the
party assumed actual, if not formal, control of Fackliga Propagandaför-

bundet [Union Propaganda Association], which had replaced the Swedish Union Opposition after its failure. Neither the party nor the Union Propaganda Association assumed any importance. The Social Democratic Party and its ally LO have dominated the development of the Swedish workers' movement.[19]

Lenin's party theory provides us with a third norm of action. During a transitional period, an enormous concentration of power in the hands of the ruling body is necessary. The vanguard of the movement is supposed to awaken the revolutionary consciousness of the workers. Not until the dictatorship of the proletariat, after the overthrow of capitalism and the bourgeois establishment, are the "armed workers" given a more independent role in the supervision and control of the planned economy, a role that is gradually strengthened. Not until then do the workers become partners in the government.

A value judgment of this norm is more difficult than in the two earlier cases because such a judgment is not a simple matter of weighing different values against each other (direct democracy versus efficiency, for example). Even if pacifist principles against the theories of violence would cause many to turn away from Leninism, as was the case with the Left Socialist minority in Sweden at the end of World War I, it is also necessary to consider the prognosis or the platform or promise that the bloody terror will be followed by the voluntary abdication of the party elite and the withering away of the apparatus of state. As is well known, opinions are divided concerning the credibility of this program.

Schumpeter and the Competition of Elites

Joseph Schumpeter's main interest was the problem of leadership. In *Capitalism, Socialism, and Democracy,* published in 1942, he indicated what in this study might be referred to as the fourth action norm for how democracies should be governed. Schumpeter agreed with Weber's view on the continuing bureaucratization of society and the repeated competition among the parties for the favor of the masses. He developed this thesis into a precise normative theory of how competition among the elites could become a guarantee against the oligarchic tendency within democratic organizations.[20]

Like Michels, Schumpeter saw the broad masses as sluggish and politically unsophisticated. The electorate hardly corresponded to the classic democratic doctrine of active, knowledgeable, and rational citizens, interested in principles. Therefore, Schumpeter assumed that most of his readers would agree with him that another democratic doctrine was now

needed, one that was more accurate and at the same time reflected what
the proponents of government by the people actually meant by democracy. The classics had wrongly assumed that the electorate had well-for-
mulated opinions about all matters and that the chosen representatives
had only to effectuate the popular opinion. Thus, the choice of representatives had become less important than the primary democratic goal of
letting the people decide political matters. But what if the two elements
were reversed? Suppose that the right of the people to decide was less
important than the selection of the representatives who have to make the
decisions? In other words, the task of the people ought to be to produce a
governing body that would have supreme responsibility in political matters. Schumpeter was very much aware of the significance of strong leadership. But he was equally cognizant that the familiar accusations of
oligarchy could be leveled at such a democratic model. He therefore
emphasized in his definition that the leaders would receive their power
in direct competition with each other for the votes of the people. This
election procedure would be the very nucleus of democracy. The elites
would keep a watchful eye on each other in open competition and thus
prevent the rise of an oligarchy.

Schumpeter's model of competitive democracy has been widely accepted in postwar political science. Adopted by leading election researchers, it has gradually become the point of departure for modern
analysis of the behavior of voters and elite groups in a democratic system. Class after class at Western universities have been taught that the
difference between democratic and nondemocratic forms of government
is not the difference between government by the people and government
by the elite, but rather that between government by several elites and
government by a single elite. In a system of several elites, competition
forces each to adapt to the wishes of the electorate, and the elite receiv-
ing the mandate is the one whose program most closely approximates the
will of the majority.

To this democratic model have been added several more or less intri-
cate theories that elite competition is not only a necessary condition for
the satisfactory functioning of a democracy but also a sufficient condition, because widespread popular participation might sometimes lead to
fanaticism and undemocratic extremism. Hitler's Germany is an example: the high level of participation showed that democracy was in a
state of crisis. According to this argument, political apathy among the
broad masses is accorded a constructive function: it preserves the
democratic form of government by allowing competition between
groups of elites.[21]

Schumpeter's model is not restricted to national systems. It has also been used in the study of several different kinds of subsystems, including labor unions. The most famous application of the theory of competition to the unions has been made by Seymour Martin Lipset. Lipset and his assistants studied the American Typographical Union, which in contrast to other American labor unions has had a two-party system for more than fifty years. According to Lipset, this arrangement has meant that a democratic system has survived, but Lipset is very cautious and his conclusions are "almost as pessimistic as those postulated by Robert Michels."[22] There are also Swedish political scientists who, referring to Michels's iron law of oligarchy and Lipset's empirical study of unions, hold the opinion that the oligarchic tendencies within the unions could be counteracted by the introduction of an internal party system with rival candidates.[23]

However, empirically oriented political science research has found Schumpeter's model difficult to use. Toward the end of the 1960s it was generally acknowledged that the attempt to decide whether politics is governed by a homogeneous "power elite" or by "competing elites" had failed. At this point, scientific interest was largely transferred to a modification of Schumpeter's model. Schumpeter thought that he had found a way to prevent oligarchy. Competition would force the elites to become representative. This representativeness, or the extent to which the views of the citizens and their leaders coincided, was measured directly. This model might be referred to as the representational model of democracy.[24] In Sweden primarily Jörgen Westerståhl, Bo Särlvik, and their students have stressed the term "concurrence of opinion" within democratic theory. They have successfully accumulated a considerable amount of material that shows the extent to which concurrence of opinion exists between the people and the elites.[25]

Schumpeter's model of democracy offers a fourth action norm for the governing of democratic organizations. Together with Michels, Weber, and Lenin, Schumpeter held the view that democracies need strong leaders. However, in contrast to Weber and Lenin, he did not propose an organization that neglected its function of popular government for other values such as efficient protection of its own interests or success for the socialist revolution. By suggesting a more realistic model than Rousseau's direct democracy, Schumpeter indicated an organization of the political process that in its simplicity is the surest guarantee against an oligarchy: the theory of competing elites. Thus, Schumpeter's model of democracy appears to many political scientists as the ultimate solution to Michels's dilemma of oligarchy within democratic organizations.

Interactive Democracy and the Public Spirit

The preceding pages are in no way intended as an exhaustive history of ideas. To discuss the governance problems of democracy in a systematic and chronological fashion would require a separate thesis. At times the theories linked with the authors have actually been formulated by their followers. The analysis has focused on some of those reactions to Michels's statement on oligarchy within workers' organizations which have seemed especially interesting in view of intellectual clarity and original- ity, ideological influence as well as applicability to present-day condi- tions within the unions. The preceding pages should thus be viewed primarily as a logical analysis of possible ways out of Michels's dilemma. By exemplifying this analysis as concretely as possible with the aid of classic authors, the wealth of aspects inherent in the question of union democracy and the powerful tradition within political theory to which it belongs have been suggested.

When the normative position of this study is presented now, that is, what will be the fifth action norm for how democratic organizations should be governed, *Folket och eliterna* [The People and the Elites], published in 1970, is the point of departure. The norm is the so-called interactive model of democracy. A key word of this model—one corre- sponding to the empirical term "oligarchy" used by Michels and to the normative terms "direct democracy," "bureaucratic efficiency," "revolu- tionary vanguard," and "competition of elites" used by Rousseau, Weber, Lenin, and Schumpeter, respectively—is the term "public spirit." Oligarchy within democratic organizations can be avoided if the interaction between leadership and membership functions in such a way as to develop the public spirit of the individual.

The new political science theories based on Schumpeter constituted a challenge to the classic democratic doctrine, according to which popular government is supported by an active citizenry. The functionalist school of political science emphasizes the elites, neglects the behavior of the masses, and holds that political apathy among the masses can benefit de- mocracy. These positions are difficult to reconcile with classic demo- cratic doctrine, in which democracy means a system that stresses the political role of the ordinary citizen in a completely different way. For while there undoubtedly were vast differences among the various politi- cal philosophers who championed the introduction of democracy during the nineteenth century, they all agreed on one point: the people, not the elites, should be the center of the new system. The revolutionary new idea of the democratic breakthrough was precisely that the popular ma- jority had finally come of age politically and had become the very foundation of political power. The democratic ideology was regarded as a radical, almost revolutionary, doctrine up to the end of World War I, when democratic ideas were put to their first serious test—and in many ways proved ineffectual. The communist and fascist regimes that followed and that also paid lip service to democracy forced democracy to assume a defensive position in order to protect the values that were now threatened by totalitarianism. Through the efforts of Schumpeter, this position received its theoretical definition, while democracy was transformed from a popular, radical theory to an elitist, defensive one. As a term, "classic democratic doctrine" will mean here the popular ideology that existed up to the outbreak of World War I.

In order for the term "public spirit" to be of practical analytical use it will be necessary to define it further. For this purpose, John Stuart Mill's work is important. The choice of Mill might appear surprising because he is often regarded as one of the leading theoreticians of representative democracy and as one who favored a dominant position for the political elite as the representatives of the people. But the existence of a representative system does not necessarily preclude the political participation of the people. Mill himself considered a representative system to be the only one capable of realizing democracy and thus the will of the people, provided that the citizens themselves were politically enlightened and interested. Democracy could best be effected through a balance between representative governing bodies and active members. Mill detailed how the activation of the members was to be achieved. Political participation of the masses was not only a goal in itself; it was also the means for a vast program of popular education. Popular participation in the decision-making process would broaden the horizons of the people, increase their sense of responsibility to include others, even those outside their immediate families, and lift their intellectual and moral life to a higher level. In short, the goal of democracy was to develop the public spirit of the individual through universal participation in the governing process. Mill's program of political education constituted his most original contribution to the development of democratic theory and has been of utmost importance in the debate on democracy.[26]

The development of public spirit is the normative postulate for the model of interactive democracy. In order for a political system to be called democratic, the interaction between leadership and membership has to be constituted in such a way that it develops the public spirit of the individual. A methodological consequence of this position is that the success of democracy is measurable by the extent to which that system has managed to further this public spirit.

The objective of the model of interactive democracy is sociopsychological: through the process of participation, the personality of an individual is changed; his acceptance of political responsibility and commitment is broadened to include the system as a whole. Participation is the means, public spirit the goal. It is thus impossible to lower the demand for participation without simultaneously reducing the possibility of success. This is the key point of difference between this theory and those of Weber, Lenin, and Schumpeter. Their theories might be questioned from an empirical point of view: maybe bureaucracy is not as efficient as Weber thought; maybe the revolution will not be followed by the classless society that Lenin visualized; maybe the competition among elites will be limited to a prearranged area more restricted in scope than that which Schumpeter foresaw so that it becomes ineffectual as a corrective against oligarchy.[27] Whether these objections are valid is not the concern here, but it is important that these norms for action do not make popular participation in the decision-making process the prerequisite for the attainment of the goal, "development of public spirit."

Opponents of the model of interactive democracy object that the politicians themselves generally do not consider the development of public spirit a fundamental democratic value. Instead, according to Jörgen Westerståhl, they have ascribed that role to the value that he singled out in his representational model, namely consensus. The debate in Sweden concerns "precisely this mirror theory , i.e., the demand that the elected assembly should mirror the opinion of the electorate. This constantly recurring idea is expressed in various ways—each vote should have the same worth, the system of election by majority is 'unfair,' etc.—and every election reform has been justified by the search for more perfect representativity."[28] Although this quotation accurately reflects current Swedish political debate, it is wrong to claim that this has always been the Swedish democratic tradition. Instead, it was precisely lofty educational ideals that inspired the fight for democracy and general suffrage among the popular movements and mass parties around the turn of the century. Whose opinion in this matter has the largest number of adherents is of no importance; majority rule cannot be invoked for scientific positions; the scientist must himself be responsible for his model. This study seeks to reawaken interest in this older and now weakened tradition, first put forth by John Stuart Mill, and postulates the development of public spirit as the normative goal of democracy. The positive value assigned to the term "public spirit" is the fixed normative point of departure for this study of the interaction between the leadership and members within the Swedish trade union movement. This is the only instance in which a value judgment will be allowed to influence the investigation.

The interactive model of democracy with public spirit as the normative postulate and the representational model with consensus as the basic value are compatible to a large extent: John Stuart Mill is the spiritual father of both. On the one hand, a relatively high degree of participation—which furthers the public spirit—becomes a condition for representativity. For if the public does not participate and formulate views, there will be no opinion for the politicians to represent (nor two opinion structures for political scientists to compare). Because participation is a condition for representativity, as it is for public spirit, Westerståhl and his assistants have devised additional ways of measuring the development of democracy, including analyses of the range of participation. On the other hand, representativity of opinion is of considerable interest as a value to those studying the model of interactive democracy. For this value constitutes a part of one of the variables used for measuring interaction between leaders and membership. The relationship between the two models becomes primarily a question of emphasis. Two different aspects of democracy are stressed in the interactive and representational models.

Although these differences should not be exaggerated, they nevertheless influenced the choice of terminology. It was necessary to select a term other than "representative democracy" to dissociate interactive democracy from representative democracy as practiced in the West during the last few decades and from Schumpeter and his followers. Practical representative democracy has always viewed the precise reflection of public interest and values as the central value. In the interactive model, the effort is directed toward developing the public spirit of the individual through general participation in the governing process.

Even if value judgments have been the guides in these choices, it might be possible also, in a discussion of representativity versus public spirit, to raise logical objections to the representational model. If representativity is postulated as the foremost democratic value, the primary duty of the politicians should be to reflect popular opinion as accurately as possible. But what happens then to the power of influence, the creation of public opinion that John Stuart Mill deemed necessary for educating the masses to a role of political responsibility? Such influence over the masses by the elite presupposes a democratic theory that neither forbids the elite to hold opinions other than those of the masses nor prevents it from attempting to sway the opinion of the general public. There is no place for this important leadership role in the representational model.[29] But elites should have an independent, opinion-forming function and in some cases be required to go against public opinion. To paraphrase Michels, it is only through propaganda, intensive at times, that the masses become politically committed and widen their views to include the system as a whole. It is assumed that public spirit exists to a greater extent among the leaders than among the general public.[30] The hypothesis that the leadership is more public spirited than the members will be applied to the Swedish trade union movement and will be of fundamental importance to the theoretical framework of this study.

The leadership is thus accorded an independent, opinion-forming role vis-à-vis the members and has not only the right but also at times the duty to go against the opinion of the membership. There exists a great difference between the model of interactive democracy and Rousseau's action norm, which precluded a leadership at all. Arguments against Rousseau's norm of action, direct democracy, can be divided into the empirical and the normative. From the empirical point of view, the chief argument against direct democracy is usually that this form of decision making is simply unable to function in larger units such as modern states or national interest organizations. Not even the modified Rousseauist principles of organization that the Left Socialists sought to apply in Sweden around 1920 proved workable. From a normative point of view, the main objection is that, like the representational model, direct democracy allows no room for creation of opinion by the leadership, a necessary condition for the development of public spirit among the citizens.

As mentioned previously Rousseau followed a very special metaphysical chain of reasoning to show how consensus can always be achieved in democratic organizations. When a society is created the individual ceases to exist and is replaced by a collective phenomenon, the general will. The idea of the general will has had some disastrous consequences in Western history. Many of the most ruthless dictators of the twentieth century, whose appearance is an anomaly in itself considering Rousseau's ideal of political equality, have declared themselves the true interpreters of the general will. They have thereby justified the right to liquidate their opponents, who have "misinterpreted the general will." What is the relationship between Rousseau's idea of the general will and the public spirit of interactive democracy? Interactive democracy assigns the leadership a strong position. Do these strong leaders then not run the risk, in their "education" of the general membership, of regarding themselves as the true proponents of the general will and thus ignore the right of the individual to form his own opinions?

From a theoretical standpoint the big difference between the terms general will and public spirit is that public spirit is not supraindividual. Public spirit within a certain group is nothing else but the attitude toward the association that the members actually express. Within the in-

teractive model of democracy there is no room for metaphysical magic
for the purpose of manipulating the views expressed by the citizens. But
even if the leadership does not apply Rousseau's advanced metaphysics,
the "educational program" to which it subjects its members might contain so much propaganda and indoctrination that it would appear irrec-
oncilable with liberal values. A practical consequence of the antiorganic
and antimetaphysical view, nowadays commonly taken for granted, is
the need to define the rules that apply to the interaction between leaders
and members during the process of opinion-formation so that the right of
expressing minority views is respected. In this study, not only majority
rule but also the principle of minority rights will be regarded as strict requirements for democracy, in defining the model of interactive democracy as it applies to the problem of governing the Swedish trade union
movement. Is Swedish union leadership successful in developing public
spirit while respecting the rights of the minorities?

According to the model of interactive democracy, the solution to Michels's dilemma is the interaction between the leaders and the led that
develops the public spirit of the individual. This action norm compared
to the classic political discourse on the organization of democratic government shows that the model of interactive democracy is an attempt to
balance a number of partly contradictory democratic values against one
another, while the other normative models seem to focus on one single
value and isolate it from the others. Thus Weber, Lenin, Schumpeter,
and the advocates of the representational model concentrate exclusively
on the behavior of the elite and argue that the elite should be efficient,
revolutionary, internally competitive, and representative of the views of
the people without having further interest in active, popular, political
participation, and the resulting stimulation of the education of the citizens. A similar vacuum can be found in Rousseau's norm for action. He
said nothing about how an organization is to champion its interests in a
political equality without leaders, or exactly how the people are to be
turned into ideal citizen-philosophers, as his theory dictates. In the interactive model, on the other hand, democratic values are explicitly tied to
both levels—leaders and membership—and the goal of democracy is said
to be the development of the public spirit of the individual through interaction between the leaders and the led.

The Functioning of Interactive Democracy

The interactive democracy model is shown in figure 1.1.[31] In *Folket och
eliterna* the presentation was divided into various analytical levels. For

Figure 1.1. The Interactive Democracy Model.

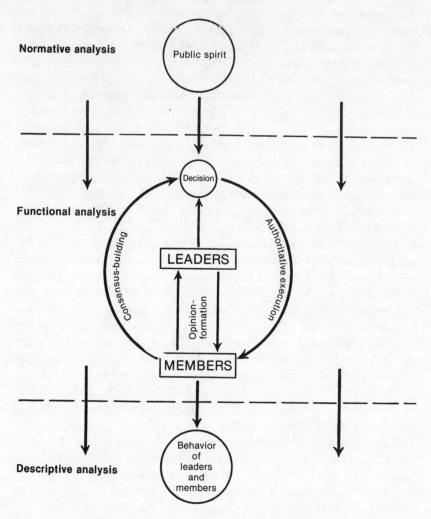

the statements proposed by the philosophers of democracy from the eighteenth-century radicals to the present-day election researchers can be divided into three broad categories. Those of the first category present factual descriptions of the political behavior of the individual voter. For example, it might be claimed that 17 percent of the voters follow the political debate in all four media included in the study (newspapers, magazines, radio, television). Statements of the second category explain the functions of the political system. For example, it might be said that the democratic system functions best if the masses involve themselves only to a limited extent in the government of a country, because a strong commitment easily leads to intolerance and extremism that might threaten democratic values. Statements that fall into the third category establish norms or guidelines for the organization of society. For example, it might be said that an effort should be made to develop the public spirit of the individual through the involvement of everybody in the national government. Thus, in this study as in *Folket och eliterna*, the same distinction among descriptive, functional, and normative levels of analysis is made.

Each of these three categories has a different theoretical status. Statements at the descriptive and functional levels describe reality—the views held by a certain union member or the functioning of a union local—and can consequently be proved or disproved through empirical fieldwork. Within the two empirical categories two differences can be discerned. The first applies to scope: to provide only a description is less ambitious an undertaking than to attempt an explanation. This distinction is sometimes difficult to maintain. But generally speaking there are clear and unmistakable differences between the descriptive and the explanatory parts of a scientific study. The second concerns the individual-system aspect: descriptive statements describe the behavior and attitudes of individual citizens or members, functional statements the function of the entire political or union-related system.

Statements at the normative analytical level contain guidelines for the organization of society. These guidelines contain value judgments or normative postulates that state which goals should be pursued. Value judgments cannot be tested scientifically; instead, the scientist has to be content with defining the values as clearly as possible and sometimes, as part of this effort, with tracing their theoretical and historical backgrounds. It is also part of the analytical process at the normative level to investigate the extent to which the recommended form of government actually leads to the desired goal.

At the functional analytical level, the model of interactive democracy is ideally thought to function as follows (see figure 1.1). "Opinion-formation" consists of an interaction between members and leadership in which, among other things, the members actively participate in the political process, gain insight into the system, and ally themselves with certain associated values. At the same time, the leaders seek to inform and propagandize the members, familiarize themselves with membership opinion, and commit themselves to a strengthening of the values of the system. The result of this process of opinion-formation is ideally "con-

sensus-building" between leadership and members, as concerns both
election procedures and other matters. Again ideally, the leadership
makes "decisions" based on the consensus promoted by this two-way
process of opinion-formation. Finally, the decisions are executed in an
"authoritative" manner. The meaning of the four variables "opinion-formation," "consensus-building," "decisions," and "authoritative execution" is further defined in table 1.1.

Opinion-formation comprises membership "activity," and is made operational by such efforts as attendance at a union meeting, the reading of
union publications, leadership involvement in union activity, or informational work. But activity is not enough. It is not even necessarily desirable. Some ideologues have stressed the value of activity more
forcefully than the theoreticians of democracy. These men have actually
been hostile to democracy, and their philosophy of activity is an expression of a vitalism and an anti-intellectualism that is alien to a democratic
way of thinking. The term "activity" therefore must be qualified in two
respects. First, activity has to be coupled with competence—"enlighten-
ment" was the motto of the classics. Membership competence refers to
such things as factual knowledge of union matters, whereas leadership
competence is indicated by awareness of opinion within the local or by
actual knowledge of the details of the agreement.

Second, activity has to include society as a whole, not just private po-

Table 1.1. Values at the Level of Functional Analysis.

| Normative Analysis | Functional Analysis | | Descriptive Analysis |
	Variable	Value	
The normative postulate of the model has been discussed on pages 16–21. It is specified in terms of the problems of union democracy on pages 53–55. Operationalizations and results are presented on pages 72–77 and 148–150.	Opinion-formation	Activity Competence System orientation	The operationalizations are presented along with the results on pages 72–111.
	Consensus-building	Legitimacy Agreement of opinion Demands Schooling	
	Decisions	Decisions Nondecisions	
	Authoritative execution	Authority	

litical advantages—"the classic civic virtue: the interest of the voters should extend to society as a whole, not only to private political advantages."[32] This attitude is defined as "system orientation," and it refers to the attitude of members and leaders alike toward the system of which they are part, the extent to which they consider themselves able to influence it, their view of majority rule, the desirability of a high degree of membership activity, and their respect for the rights of the minority. The normative analysis stressed the importance of establishing careful guidelines for the respect of minority rights; this is especially significant if a model is to establish civic education as the goal of democracy, while it seeks to protect the freedom of opinion of the individual. The extent to which the rights of the minority are respected within the Swedish trade union movement will be studied with the aid of the value "system orientation" measured in several ways.

The first value in consensus-building, the second variable of the model, is "legitimacy." Originally it was "competition." However, competition cannot be viewed as a sufficient condition for democracy, and may not even constitute a necessary condition, especially because the liberal demand for the respect of minority rights can be satisfied through other values in the model. Exactly what is safeguarded by stating that leaders should be chosen in open competition? The construction of an election procedure the outcome of which the members can accept because they view it as the result of a fair contest and not of the plotting of some power elite is a direct attempt to avoid a situation of oligarchy. However, it does happen that the membership accepts an election procedure that includes only one candidate for a position, or rejects an election procedure even if there is open competition. Therefore, in this study members were asked simply if they found the election procedure acceptable, and the question of whether systems with a competitive election procedure are more legitimate than systems without competition was left open. However, this question will be tested empirically.

The next value in the consensus-building variable is "agreement of opinion," or representativity. Another difficulty in connection with this term is whether the consensus that the elites are attempting to create within the system is "true," the expression of the carefully considered opinion of the members, or "false," the result of manipulation by the elites. It has hitherto proved difficult to decide scientifically whether an agreement of opinion between leadership and members is true or false. In order to render the terms "true agreement" and "false agreement-manipulation" empirically useful, new techniques of operation are needed.[33]

Before discussing the next value, "demands," the final value, "schooling," which might also be called education or socialization, will be discussed. Does participation further public spirit and related values, and if so, how? How do the union leaders view their leadership role, and do they feel duty-bound to go against the opinion of the membership at times, or do they view their role as a direct mirror of that opinion?

In contrast to the three values "legitimacy," "agreement of opinion," and "schooling," the value "demands" has no counterpart in *Folket och eliterna.*[34] It has now been included because earlier research into trade union democracy in Sweden had shown that the most active members are those who are dissatisfied with the results of union activity and that, paradoxically, these members, unhappy with the contract agreement, are often the most favorably inclined toward the labor union movement.[35] Against this background, how should the role of dissatisfaction in the democratic process be viewed? In the 1956 debate on the budget, Tage Erlander, then prime minister, commented about "the dissatisfaction of unfulfilled expectations." According to Erlander, a new kind of dissatisfaction had replaced the old one that reflected a country of poverty; this new dissatisfaction resulted because the increased expectations in a prosperous Sweden were not fulfilled rapidly enough. This discontent drove the leadership to advance the positions of the workers' movement.[36] However, to consider dissatisfaction as an asset should not be limited to the case of the unions or the workers' movement. It should be a general asset for democracy when citizens, no longer satisfied with their living conditions, place demands on the leadership for better policies. Thus, the addition of this value to the model must be seen as a dividend resulting from the continuing exchange between empirical research and normative theory.[37]

These last two values taken together illustrate how interaction between leadership and members is to function in the interactive model. When demands are formulated, stress is placed on membership participation in the government; the dissatisfaction of the members forces the system to conduct an increasingly advanced policy. Schooling emphasizes the role of the leadership. Through the influence of the leadership, after individual demands have been weighed, the members are made to accept the policy most beneficial to the system as a whole.

Before discussing the variable decision it must be emphasized once more that this model dictates indirect rather than direct democracy. Decisions are made by the elite, not by the people. But the decisions have to reflect consensus between members and leaders, both in election procedures and in factual matters, and, ideally, this consensus should have been arrived at through interaction during the process of opinion-formation.

The decision variable is dichotomous: it assumes two values, "decision" and "nondecision." These terms are taken from a theory advanced by two American political scientists who criticized the use of the concept of competition within political theory.[38] They have pointed to methodological insufficiencies in the usual analytical studies of the decision-making process that concern the question whether competing elites or a homogeneous power elite are found in the West today. In their view, it is not necessary to ask whether group conflicts have arisen on issues that have been decided. Instead, it is important to study questions that have not been discussed and subsequently decided. The hypothesis is that the elites limit competition to a few narrowly defined areas where their own interests are not threatened and that questions which may jeopardize the system are never taken up and thus become objects of "nondecision." However, the "decision-nondecision" concept has also proved difficult to use: Can the absence of something be measured?

With regard to trade unions, do the various units within that movement make decisions after a consensus has been reached, or does the leadership choose not to pursue certain questions? If the latter is the case, what considerations have been the deciding factors (respect for outside groups such as the union hierarchy, employers, the state)? A local does not have complete sovereignty, but is bound in its decisions by rather narrow judicial and economic limits. To what extent do they prevent the union movement from vigorously pursuing decisions in accordance with the expressed interest of the membership? In this connection, it is important to study whether or not a conflict between a given unit, for example, a local, and the central leadership is caused by the local's holding views and wishes that are different from those of the majority of the rank and file. If this were so, the central leadership would be representative of the membership as a whole, but not of the dissident local. This kind of analysis of nondecision carries Michels's thesis of oligarchy within the workers' organizations to an extreme.[39]

The last variable of the model is authoritative execution. In defining this concept there is need for only one value, "authority." Briefly, the union leadership enjoys authority if it is able to act upon the decisions made without encountering protests from the members. In order to make operational this general statement for analytical use in this study, it is necessary to set forth some of the conditions for making the concept of authority measurable. First, an apparent conflict exists between the values "demands" and "authority." Although dissatisfaction among members is a democratic asset spurring the leadership into action, the members should accept without protest the way in which the leadership executes the decisions. Such endorsement has to be qualified by the dissatisfaction. Second, the concept of authority must be measured in such a way that it will be clearly separate from the value "legitimacy." Throughout the history of political theory legitimacy and authority appear as twin values, often confused by the political scientists to the bewilderment of the readers. Legitimacy means that the system is acceptable to the membership because it elects the leadership in a fair and procedurally acceptable way; authority signifies that union policy is approved because the leadership has convincingly argued its case.

Between the various conditions governing the measurement of the authority variable there exist intimate bonds that further illustrate how the interaction between leadership and members is thought to function in an interactive democracy. If the members find a system legitimate, they will approve the transfer of power to the leadership for a limited period, because this may be the best way to achieve their demands. But no leadership can fulfill the wishes of all the voters. The leaders must therefore turn to the voters once more, answer their demands, and present arguments in favor of what they consider the best possible, realistic, and attainable alternative. Through such a process of interaction, the leaders can lay claim to authority and manage to gain the confidence of the rank and file for its policies.

Like all the other norms of action, with the exception of Rousseau's, the model of interactive democracy assigns to the elites an important role in the decision-making process. They are considered indispensable both for the long-term development of democracy and its goals and for its everyday functions. But in contrast to these other norms, political participation by the people assumes a central role. The people are no longer limited to serving as the ultimate legitimation of elites whom others have described as efficient regulators of interests, revolutionary propagandists, surveillants of competition, or representatives of the views of the electorate—briefly an active elite representing the interests and wishes of the passive masses. The interactive model of democracy is intended to diminish the political apathy of the people and spur the citizens to interaction with their leaders. Such interaction is not an end in itself. The normative objective is the development of public spirit in the individual.

2

The Governance of
Swedish Trade Unions

The present-day labor union movement is the offspring of industrialism and thus is a relative newcomer in Sweden, a country that remained unaffected by the industrial revolution until the 1890s—later than other European countries. Although craft unions existed after the abolition of the guilds in the mid-1800s, these associations were in no way radical organizations that directed the struggle against employers and existing society; nor was their goal total membership affiliation. With the arrival of industrialism, however, the battle cries of socialist agitation began to be heard. Since socialist and union propaganda went hand in hand, a number of trade unions were founded, and in 1898 LO was established. LO has developed into the most influential labor organization in Sweden; it has no real competition for organizing industrial workers; the white-collar unions were founded at a much later date.

The present study of trade union democracy is limited to LO and its affiliated unions and locals. Therefore, the term "labor union movement" is used here to denote LO and its components.

Union-Related Phenomena

A glance at the development of the organizational structure (30)[1] of the union movement reveals three distinct tendencies: an increase in membership, a transfer of ever greater power to the central LO leadership, and a trend toward larger and more powerful units through the process of consolidation.

Almost from the very beginning, the Swedish trade unions were governed according to the principles of representative democracy. This contrasts with the pattern of union development in Britain, the birthplace of industrialism. According to the famous account by Sidney and Beatrice Webb,[2] an extremely direct and primitive form of democracy originally prevailed in the unions of that country, a form of government that in their opinion would lead either to powerlessness and disintegration or to the uncontrolled exercise of power by a few. In Sweden, moreover, representative democracy was not limited to the local unions, and from the beginning considerable power was delegated to nationwide organizations representing the different trades.[3] These organizations achieved a position of dominance over the local unions, as witnessed, for example, by their control of strike funds because the locals were considered too weak to build up the necessary resources. Soon cooperation between a local and the central leadership was a necessary prerequisite for any effective strike action. LO, the central organization, was founded as a rather weak cynosure, and its primary duties were to gather statistics and to support defensive actions. However, when employers formed a highly centralized organization, Svenska arbetsgivareföreningen [SAF, Swedish Employers' Confederation], in 1902, a reciprocal concentration of power within the trade union movement seemed necessary. Power moved up to the next level: from locals to national unions, from national unions to the central LO leadership.

The first centrally conducted negotiations between LO and SAF led to the so-called December Compromise in 1906 in which SAF recognized the right of the workers to unionize, while LO accepted the right of the employer to choose his employees freely, and to direct the work. Within a short period, the labor union movement had managed to establish itself as a publicly recognized institution.

In order to increase the unions' power against the employers, the LO leadership championed a move from craft to industrial unions, where the workers within one industry would be organized by one single LO union to prevent the employers from pitting the interests of different unions against each other. Similarly, LO favored the consolidation of a large number of unions. An organizational plan was adopted at the LO Congress of 1912 for the consolidation of some forty unions of that time, within and outside of LO, into a total of twenty-two industrial unions. The number of members increased dramatically from 38,000 in 1899 to 186,000 in 1907.

In 1909 the successful development of LO was checked by its defeat in the general strike. There was widespread dissatisfaction with LO's cautious wage strategy, a discontent fanned by the Social Democratic Party. In several cases, the LO leadership had persuaded local workers' organizations to accept wage settlements over the objections of their members. When SAF threatened a lockout during the summer of 1909, the LO leadership felt compelled to proclaim a general strike out of fear of what many angry and combative unions might do. The outcome was a total defeat for LO. Half the membership was lost, the centralization process was interrupted, and the LO leadership ceased interfering in the conflicts of the unions.

Not until 1917 did LO attain the same membership as it had enjoyed in 1907. Then followed a new spurt in growth. In 1930 membership was 554,000, and in 1945 it reached 1,107,000. The process of centralizing the power in the hands of the leadership was resumed. Again, the relationship to the opponent on the labor market was of decisive importance. In 1936, for the first time since 1909, central wage negotiations between LO and SAF were initiated leading to the so-called Saltsjöbaden Agreement of 1938. Under this agreement the parties created a kind of voluntary judicial procedure in order to avoid both state interference in the labor market—regulating, among other things, third-party rights—and conflicts that might pose a threat to society. The Saltsjöbaden Agreement and the many decades of peaceful management-labor relations made possible by it have made Sweden a social model with strong traditions of order and justice. The centralistic tendency contained in the agreement was codified in a far-reaching revision in 1941. Henceforth, LO was "to exercise the central leadership over the efforts of the trade union movement to safeguard the interests of the wage-earners."[4]

The consolidation process was slower than expected. For there were groups, often highly skilled and highly paid, who were convinced that they would stand to lose from a merger and who tried to prevent it. The organization plan of 1912 was never realized, nor was a new plan proposed in 1926, the goal of which was a total number of thirty-three unions. By the Congress of 1931 none of the mergers outlined in the plan of 1926 had taken place. Some consolidations were made during the 1930s, but the total number of unions increased nevertheless because of membership expansion. The additions were partly the result of a greater degree of organization within the old unions, partly the result of new unions admitted to LO. In the early 1950s the LO Congress approved a plan that included thirty-eight affiliates. The actual number was forty-four during the decade, however. Throughout this period, the LO leadership quietly urged consolidation and supported those unions in favor of merger, but refrained from coercion. "The gentle attitude which was expressed already by the 1903 Congress has come to characterize the actions of the LO leadership toward the unions in question ever since."[5]

The rapid membership growth has continued during the postwar period. In 1974, when the fieldwork for this study was completed, LO had 1,863,481 members, or an affiliation rate of 90 percent, a very high figure

by international standards. As for mergers, the numerous economic ratio-
nalizations of the 1960s provided a somewhat belated breakthrough.
After a standstill since the 1940s, a number of consolidations took place
during the 1960s. In 1966 LO recommended a total of twenty-two—the
same number as had been proposed in 1912. In 1974 the actual total was
twenty-five. These affiliates, as well as their membership figures in 1974,
are indicated in table 2.1.

The transition in the mid-1950s from separate union negotiations to
central wage negotiations between LO and SAF proved to be of para-
mount importance for conditions within the labor union movement and
the labor market. The employers had already favored central negotiations; LO was now able to balance the interests of different member

Table 2.1. Membership in National Unions, 1974.

Union	Number of Members
Agricultural Workers	11,796
Building Maintenance Workers	33,649
Building Workers	162,563
Chimney Sweeps	1,289
Electricians	26,686
Factory Workers	99,944
Food Workers	53,917
Forest Workers	24,242
Garment Workers	56,382
Graphic Industry Workers	38,941
Hairdressers	3,986
Hotel and Restaurant Workers	26,779
Metal Workers	443,700
Miners	13,662
Municipal Workers	309,121
Musicians	9,025
Painters	23,154
Pulp and Paper Workers	49,641
Seamen	15,200
Sheet Metal Workers	4,824
State Employees	174,788
Transport Workers	50,231
Commercial Employees	133,310
Social Insurance Employees	17,021
Wood Industry Workers	79,630
Total	1,863,481

Source: *LO Statistics*, 1974 (Stockholm, 1974), p. 37.

groups against each other so that a more equitable agreement could be reached. In today's centralized wage negotiations, after extensive polling of the membership for its opinion and exhaustive analysis of economic developments, three persons from LO conduct the bargaining at the decisive stage with three representatives from SAF. Any agreement made there must first be ratified by both a larger bargaining delegation and the unions. The agreement is then effected at the local level, where negotiations and contracts may be necessary to fit specific conditions. This bargaining structure has further concentrated power in the hands of the LO leadership, and has resulted in a large bureaucracy of experts and fact finders within the top levels of the organization.

In the 1960s, merger was an attractive option at several levels of the union hierarchy. The structural changes in the economy and the steadily growing tasks of the union movement made consolidation desirable also at the local level. In order to increase resources, locals in adjacent communities were merged into so-called district branches. This consolidation process has been rapid and far-reaching: the number of locals has decreased from 8,950 in 1948, the peak year, to 1,897 in 1974. Figures for the consolidation of locals, for membership, and for the number of unions during the postwar period will be found in table 2.2, and a schematic representation of the organizational structure of the Swedish trade union movement will be found in figure 2.1.

The LO leadership was fully aware of the strain on union democracy brought on by this transition to district branches. A number of measures were taken to lessen these risks as much as possible. Thus, the old locals remained as sections of the new district branches. It was further recommended that the branches introduce a system of representational bodies

Table 2.2. LO-Affiliated Members, Locals, and Unions (postwar period).

Year	Members	Locals	Unions
1945	1,106,917	8,622	46
1950	1,278,409	8,886	44
1955	1,384,456	8,739	44
1960	1,485,735	7,930	44
1965	1,564,614	5,193	38
1970	1,680,135	2,448	29
1974	1,863,481	1,897	25

Source: *LO Statistics,* 1974 (Stockholm, 1974), pp. 34–35.

Figure 2.1. Organizational Structure of the Trade Union Movement (M = members; S = sections; R = representational body; L = local committee).

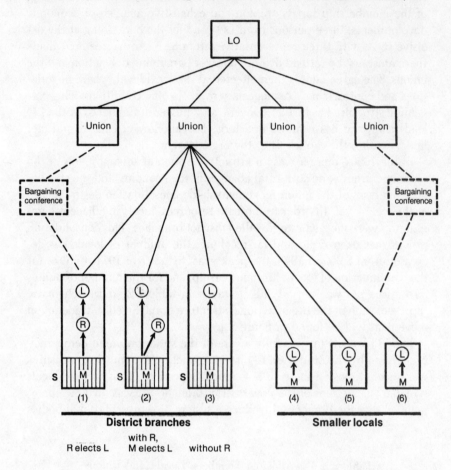

through which various membership groups were guaranteed representation in order to minimize the possible impact of occasional opinions. Not all of the district branches have followed this recommendation. In some of the branches that have done so, the representational bodies elect the branch leadership; in others the leadership is elected directly by the members. The bargaining conferences, the decisions of which are advisory, are held by the national union leadership with workers' representatives from various collective bargaining areas. Because one union can be subject to several collective agreements, it can also have several different bargaining conferences. Approximately ten unions, among them the

Building Workers, Metal Workers, and State Employees, have bargaining councils as an alternative to bargaining conferences. These councils are appointed for the duration of a congressional period; as a rule, the conferences are more temporary. The structure of the locals may vary considerably from place to place. Their membership figures also vary to a large extent, from ten members in some locals of the Agricultural Workers' Union, for example, to several thousand members in some locals of the Metal Workers' Union, actually as many as some of the smaller consolidated district branches with a section system. However, the smaller locals are still quite common.

The transition to district branches, still far from complete, constitutes one of the main issues in the debate of recent years on trade union democracy. What is the attitude of trade unionists to the district branch reform (31) now that some observations based on experience can be made? Has membership influence decreased, as has sometimes been maintained, and have the members thus become more critical of the trade union movement? Or has the system of sections and representational bodies, greater resources for the local, smoother negotiations, and better contacts with the national union created a more positive attitude?

The critics of union centralization maintain that the leaders of the large locals of today are not acquainted with the members (10) nor do they know membership opinion (12).

Furthermore, echoing Michels's criticism of trade union oligarchy, they state that the members of the enormous unions of today lack trust in the local and section leaderships (19), that they distrust their full-time representatives (ombudsmen) (18), whom they view as civil servants rather than as workers from their own background, and that they especially distrust the top officials (17). Because power is concentrated in the central leadership in the name of democracy, the critics argue that, with central negotiations, representatives, and leadership at different levels, the system of representation (16) itself has been compromised and should be abolished. Such observations concerning worker reaction to centralization are frequently encountered in the debate on the union movement. They take for granted a centralized, boss-run organization. However, it is reasonable to ask: Does bossism (23) exist in the Swedish labor union movement today?

In order to attempt an answer the question must be further defined: What is actually meant by "bossism"? From the viewpoint of the critics, bossism means a condition in which the duly elected trade union officials no longer represent membership opinion, but conduct some other policy, often with the tacit understanding of the employers, or of a Social Democratic government of excessively bourgeois leanings. To what extent does representativity of opinion exist between the membership, local committees, and the central LO leadership? In analyzing this question, it is important to remember that a local committee or the LO leadership can be perfectly representative of the membership at large while not being representative of a single local that might have interests of its own different from those of other locals. To what extent are the differences of opinion between a group of members and the central leadership caused by the former having different interests from those of the majority?

Thus, the absence of bossism must mean that the central leadership is representative of the majority but not necessarily of every single union local. According to the principles of democracy, the minority, even if it constitutes 100 percent of a given local, must yield to the majority. In addition, other limiting factors are imposed on the locals by structures outside the jurisdiction of the labor union movement: the employer, the state, the general economic picture. Whether rooted in the internal organizational structure of a centralized union movement or in the economic and political oppression mechanisms of the external capitalist system, these various limiting factors are basically unacceptable to a revolutionary. Consequently, the extreme Left demanded: "Make the trade union a fighting organization!" (28). The context seems to suggest that local leaders should primarily support membership interests without regard either for union coordination, which tends to weaken the workers' position in the struggle against the employer, or for regulations and circumstances invoked by the state or the employer. Such obstacles should be removed instead by wildcat strikes or similar actions. If LO limits the freedom of action of its members, it should be reorganized. The trade union movement should take up the wishes of the membership and pass resolutions that are in the interest of the workers. To what extent does the decision-making process at various union levels correspond to these demands for a fighting organization?

The far-reaching centralization within the union movement has also brought with it extensive professionalization. Thus, a position of leadership within the union has become the starting point for a career within the trade union movement, the Social Democratic Party, or the state bureaucracy rather than a temporary position of trust to be handed over, after a period of time, to a fellow worker. According to the critics, this development should have lessened membership trust in the trade union movement. But what impact has professionalization had on elected representatives at various levels? To what extent are candidates motivated to pursue leadership positions out of idealism (20) in order to work for improved conditions for the workers, and to what extent are elected positions nothing but a springboard for launching a private career? To what extent are the principles of democracy applied in union elections (22)? Are they run in such a way that the members are actually able to judge the candidates rationally, or do they in practice mean a routine vote of confidence for committee members? How much time do present-day committee members devote to union-related work (6)? With how many members do they discuss (7) union issues during a normal work week? How often do they provide information (8) to the membership concerning union matters in union-sponsored meetings at the place of work or elsewhere? How competent are the union officials when it comes to following the increasingly complicated judicial and economic regulations of working life, and how fully and completely do they understand the text of an agreement (11)? What is their attitude toward membership activity (21)? Do they fear that an increase in membership activity will curtail the tasks of the elected officials and representatives, or do they view the present-day low level of membership activity as one of the most serious problems demanding the attention of the labor union movement today? On the other hand, do the elected officials have any real conception of leadership (27)? For interactive democracy wants not passive puppets of the popular will, but leaders actively influencing and forming opinions.

What then does this development toward centralization and professionalization hope to achieve? In its most important area of activity, wage policy, LO usually lists the following three objectives: (1) to secure for the wage earners a reasonable share of the national income; (2) to create equitable wage relationships for different groups; and (3) to monitor the effects of wage developments on the national economy. In an authoritative pamphlet, Rudolf Meidner and Berndt Öhman, two economists close to LO, comment on this program: "A cursory glance at official LO documents, i.e. reports, congressional minutes, and statements made by union leaders, will show that the first objective quoted has not been one of the main issues for many decades."[6] The fight for higher wages is the classic function of the trade union movement. To give added support to these demands and to prevent employers from pitting different membership interests against each other the centralization process was initiated already before the turn of the century. The authors stress that because the specter of unemployment has been avoided at the same time that the strength of the union movement has grown, the labor movement has been able to advance its positions at the expense of capital. Thus, the first objective has not been the center of heated debates of the last few decades. "The criticism heard for example at the LO Congresses of the forties and fifties, that the leadership had neglected this part of their task, was always measured, not to say tame, and it was always countered with

convincing figures showing the increased share of the national income
constituted by wages. This criticism ceased almost completely during the
sixtics."[7] Instead, the two other objectives have become the center of discussion. "The characteristic trait of the Swedish trade union movement
. . . is its deep engagement in the problem of distribution within the
wage-earner collective and its attempts to view wage policy from the aspect of the general socioeconomic picture."[8]

Such efforts are usually referred to as a wage policy of solidarity (1),
which has its origins in the socialist ideology of solidarity. From the very
beginning, the Swedish labor movement supported the idea that the
lowest-paid workers ought to receive extra support from the movement.
During the 1930s these aims were further accentuated. In a motion to
the LO Congress in 1936 the Metal Workers' Union endorsed a move to a
"socialist wage policy (of solidarity)," a move that presupposed a more
influential role for LO in the negotiations.[9] A committee was appointed
and its recommendation that LO be granted the central direction of
wage policy in order to work toward such a solidarity was enacted in the
revision of bylaws in 1941.[10]

World War II resulted in a setback for many of the points of the union
wage policy program. LO was criticized for all but ignoring the wage
policy of solidarity. After the war, when many expected the working
class to achieve its goals, inflation, a new phenomenon in Sweden, struck
and created new obstacles. LO was forced to agree to a wage freeze out
of consideration for general economic stability, even though, in the long
run, such a control is unacceptable to a labor union movement. At that
point a solution was presented by two economists in LO's department of
economic research, a solution which was to prove of utmost importance
to the shaping both of LO's wage policy and of the economic policy of
the nation as a whole. In a series of articles and pamphlets, Gösta Rehn
and Rudolf Meidner pointed out[11] that in a society of full employment
not only wages but also profits rose. The expectations of a permanent
economic boom produced competition in industry for the work force
through which profits were to be realized. Thus, in addition to the general negotiated raises, there was a considerable wage drift triggered by
industrial competition in the area of wages. The economic policy therefore should aim at minimizing profits, so that the devastating wage competition would cease. This would be achieved through high wages and
high taxes, two economic and political methods used to facilitate the
ideological objectives of the Social Democrats of raising the living standard of the industrial worker and of increasing the power of the state
over the economic sphere.

Gösta Rehn was well aware that lower profits would also mean that private enterprise would not be able to maintain production and employment levels in all areas. This afforded the Social Democratic government an opportunity for greater influence over the economy; according to the tradition established in the 1930s, the state should step in whenever private enterprise failed. State-run enterprise presented one possible solution, but Rehn's recommendation of a new, active labor market policy to move workers, after retraining, from inefficient low-paying industries to efficient high-wage enterprises was far more promising. This proposed labor market policy would be not merely a solution to the dilemma of inflation—high wages—but also a continuation of the positive, efficiency-oriented attitude of the Social Democrats toward rapid structural change and progressive ideas in the economic sector. Rehn stressed that his proposal meant a step in the direction of the egalitarian vision of socialism. The retraining program was to be of such magnitude that everyone would be allowed to select the most suitable and best-paying job. The definitive evidence that LO adopted Rehn's theories was the report entitled *The Labor Union Movement and Full Employment* submitted before the LO Congress in 1951.[12]

During the economic decline of the late 1950s, the new labor market policy was introduced with a new sense of purpose. By now this policy has become an international model and today constitutes the chief economic and political program of the Social Democratic Party. Although it was a strong contributory factor in the rapid economic change during the 1960s, toward the end of that decade it was criticized. Many workers were forced to relocate against their will because some areas were totally devoid of employment possibilities. To help alleviate this problem, a localization policy was introduced which sought to regulate the establishment of new industry by taking into account the employment situation of the area in question. Rehn's theories still constitute the fundamental principles governing the attitude of the Social Democrats and the trade unions toward inflation, industrial profits, wages, state regulation of the economy, taxes, job market policy, and equalization of income.[13]

From the very beginning there were those who doubted that this new policy would bring about an equalization of income. The policy of relocation and retraining could surely never become so effective that all low-income employees would change employment. According to some, there was a risk that the new job market policy would exacerbate the problem of low wages because it favored expansion-oriented enterprises that could pay higher than average wages.[14] The spirit of radicalism that was prevalent during the 1960s and the increased availability of data concerning low-income employees served to heighten impatience over the slow pace of income equalization. Starting in 1969, LO therefore pursued a vigorous policy to raise the incomes of low-wage employees during the central wage negotiations, and a considerable share of the resources earmarked for bargaining was set aside for this policy. LO has pursued a policy of equalizing incomes with great consistency and sense of purpose in all subsequent negotiations.

LO economists had thus tried to tackle the problem of postwar inflation. Nevertheless, as this problem persisted, LO found itself forced to agree to a wage freeze. The successful enforcement of such a drastic measure demanded strict exercise of LO's authority. It is against this background that the move to centrally conducted negotiations in 1956 should be viewed. Central negotiations proved to be vitally important to the question of low wages. In order to present a unified trade union movement during central negotiations, added emphasis was placed on affinity, solidarity, and equalization; thus, the prime factors behind the move to central bargaining were socioeconomic. The wage policy of solidarity was a direct result of this centralization.[15]

How high are industrial wages (32) and how have they changed in later years? Largely as a result of the research departments of SAF and LO, a wealth of statistical material is now available, illustrating wage developments within different trades, industries, agreement areas, and unions. Within the LO collective, the distribution of wages in 1974 is indicated in table 2.3. The levels vary from one industry to another, with an average hourly wage of 21.32 Swedish crowns for men and 17.86

Table 2.3. Average Hourly Industrial Wage, 1974 (Swedish crowns).

Industry	Men	Women
Mining	23.96	20.78
Manufacturing	21.26	17.85
Food, beverage, and tobacco	20.57	17.50
Wood products	19.90	17.81
Textile, clothing, and leather	19.12	16.30
Pulp, paper, and paper products; graphic	23.26	18.90
Chemical, petroleum, rubber, and plastics	20.27	17.58
Earth and stone products	20.59	17.66
Iron, steel, and metal	22.69	20.66
Mechanical	21.24	18.53
Other manufacturing	19.57	17.02
Mining and manufacturing	21.32	17.86

Source: Central Office of Statistics, Department of Labor Market Statistics (Stockholm, 1974).

Table 2.4. Hourly Industrial Wage for Women, 1950–1970 (percentage of men's wages).

Industry	1950	1960	1965	1970
Mining	48	48	64	83
Metal and mechanical	71	71	81	84
Earth and stone	68	66	71	80
Pulp and paper	76	70	76	80
Wood	76	78	83	87
Graphic	62	68	69	72
Food	72	77	79	82
Beverage and tobacco	77	82	85	89
Textile and clothing	76	78	80	84
Leather, fur, and rubber	71	72	75	82
Chemical	68	72	76	82
All industries	71	69	75	80

Source: Lennart Nyström, *Löner och priser* (Stockholm: Tiden, 1972), p. 40.

Swedish crowns for women. Women still earn less than men, but as table 2.4 shows, the gap has narrowed substantially during the postwar period; in 1950, women's wages constituted 71 percent of those of men; in 1960, 69 percent; in 1965, 75 percent; and in 1970, 80 percent.

A wage policy of solidarity has been the officially stated objective of LO for several decades. Thus, it is interesting to view wage development over a period of time. Figure 2.2 shows the development and change in wage spread from 1959 to 1974. In this figure the statistics have been di-

Figure 2.2. Wage Spread, 1959–1974: SAF-LO Agreement Areas Relative to Average Wage Level. From *Tvärsnitt*, p. 54, and *LOs verksamhetsberättelse* (Stockholm, 1974), p. 86.

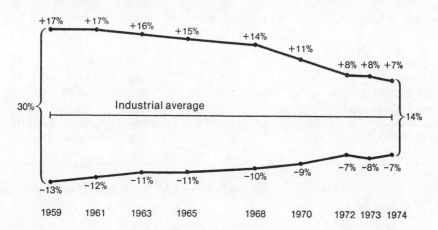

vided by agreement areas below and above the industrial average; then
with a view toward the great variation in numbers of affected wage
earners within the different agreement areas the relative wage level has
been weighed against the number of working hours. The figure indicates
a distinct leveling off, with this tendency accentuated after 1969 when
the vigorous efforts to deal with the low-wage question at the bargaining
table were initiated.[16]

Despite the leveling tendencies, there still exists a significant wage
spread in Sweden. The results of a questionnaire distributed by LO's research department in 1973 shows the wage spread between different
unions (see table 2.5). The average hourly wage in 1972 was 16.10 Swed-

Table 2.5. Wage Spread among LO-Affiliated Unions, 1972.[a]

Union	Annual Income (Sw. cr.)	Standard Deviation (Sw. cr.)	Hourly Income (Sw. cr.)	Standard Deviation (Sw. öre)
Agricultural Workers	29,400	520	14.52	45
Building Maintenance Workers	32,000	960	14.38	36
Building Workers	35,150	490	18.05	29
Chimney Sweeps	37,100	670	17.45	21
Electricians	37,100	770	18.04	39
Factory Workers	29,850	530	14.48	19
Food Workers	31,550	750	15.20	37
Forest Workers	32,100	830	16.45	42
Garment Workers	24,900	690	12.88	42
Graphic Industry Workers	36,950	690	17.92	30
Hairdressers	23,500	420	11.58	23
Hotel and Restaurant Workers	24,750	860	12.81	27
Metal Workers	31,950	240	15.58	10
Miners	36,300	700	18.01	33
Municipal Workers	32,300	350	15.78	16
Painters	39,950	1,550	19.29	61
Pulp and Paper Workers	33,900	490	16.43	35
Sheet Metal Workers	34,850	790	17.43	33
State Employees	35,400	290	18.04	19
Transport Workers	34,450	690	16.80	36
Commercial Employees	28,700	480	14.46	21
Social Insurance Employees	33,650	1,560	15.81	45
Wood Industry Workers	30,400	390	14.80	18
LO total	33,200	120	16.10	6

Source: *LO-enkäten, 1973* (Stockholm: Tiden, 1973), pp. 45–46.

a. The Musicians' and Seamen's unions are excluded from our sample. They do not appear
in this table.

ish crowns. Painters, construction workers, electricians, state employees, and miners were all in the high-income bracket. In the low-income bracket were primarily barbers, hotel and restaurant employees, and garment workers. The category of unions with low-income members also includes maintenance workers, commercial employees, factory workers, agricultural workers, and workers within the wood industry.

In spite of LO's vigorous wage policy, there still exists among the membership a feeling of union dissatisfaction (24) for not achieving greater wage increases. By maintaining a policy of higher wages and equalization of wages among industrial workers while considering the general economic balance, LO is accused of pursuing too cautious a wage policy, which in practice favors capitalist interests at the expense of the workers. How widespread is this dissatisfaction among the membership with the results of the wage policy? Which groups are most dissatisfied? Does dissatisfaction run deepest among low-income employees, who objectively speaking have greater cause for complaint, or among high-income workers, who stand to lose from the equalization efforts? How is the wage policy of solidarity viewed? Does it find its greatest support among low-income earners, who have the most to gain from it? What is the position of high-income earners on the wage policy of solidarity? In what way does membership dissatisfaction contribute to the vitality of union democracy? Within the trade union movement, what issues have been neglected (25), and what demands considered important by the membership are largely ignored by the trade union movement?

Dissatisfaction with the results of the wage policy is sometimes so widespread that the members of some local or section resort to wildcat strikes (29), actions in violation of the contract. How frequent are they? What usually triggers them? Which groups are engaged in these strikes? The success of a wage policy of solidarity suggests the question whether the wave of strikes during the 1970s has been triggered by a reaction by the high-income groups against the equalization policy (see table 2.6 containing data from available negotiating agreement areas). The high-wage groups find their interests pushed aside in favor of those of the low-income groups in one bargaining session after another. The former are prevented by the central LO leadership from availing themselves of the increase in wages that the market actually would support. Many observers maintain that this puts too much strain on solidarity in the long run and that this is the reason behind the wildcat strikes. Others deny such a connection and say that it is still the traditionally disadvantaged groups, the low-income employees, who resort to strikes. "The surprising thing is not that a number of groups in profitable industries have ex-

Table 2.6. Wildcat Strikes within the Metal Workers' Union and Foundry Workers' Union, 1949–1974.

Year	Wildcat Strikes	Year	Wildcat Strikes
1949	16	1962	18
1950	11	1963	28
1951	15	1964	28
1952	10	1965	15
1953	6	1966	19
1954	10	1967	4
1955	13	1968	10
1956	14	1969	21
1957	18	1970	73
1958	10	1971	37
1959	14	1972	27
1960	21	1973	22
1961	12	1974	105

Sources: Walter Korpi, "Vilda strejker inom Metall och verkstadsindustrin" (mimeographed, Stockholm, 1968), p. 31; Johan von Holten, "Löne-frågor orsak till 90 procent av alla avtalsstridiga strejker," Arbetsgivaren no. 28, 1975, p. 4.

pressed their dissatisfaction through unauthorized strikes. The surprising thing is rather that these strikes have been limited in scope, and that the majority of high income groups, that is, groups above the industrial average, loyally have supported a wage policy of solidarity, and made possible an equalization within the LO sector."[17] The data in support of these statements are questionable. As indicated in table 2.6, the figure for 1974, compared to previous years, is extremely high. From the point of view of democratic theory it is interesting to note that the large-scale Rousseauist revolt against the elite took place at approximately the same time within the workers' organizations and the universities: the great mining conflict in the winter of 1969–70 was to labor what the student revolts were to the educational system.

It is sometimes said that the wildcat strikes are Communist-inspired. Is this true? Political party preferences (37), in general, in the locals and in the upper echelons of the union hierarchy will be examined. The Swedish labor union movement is traditionally and closely associated with the Social Democratic Party. As is seen in table 2.7, it is even difficult to find locals where the leadership is not 100 percent Social Democratic. Of the

Table 2.7. The Trade Union Movement and Political Party Preferences (percentages).

Local steering committees, 1973 (N = 1,738)[a]	
Social Democratic	97.4
Communist	2.2
Non-socialist	0.3
Politically independent	0.1
Voting by industrial workers, 1973 (N = 846, selective sample)	
Social Democratic	64
Communist	6
Non-socialist	22
Nonvoting	8
Collective affiliation, 1974 (N = 1,897 locals, 981,778 members)	
Collectively affiliated locals	40
Nonaffiliated locals	60
Collectively affiliated members	73
Individually affiliated members	27

Sources: Figures for the local steering committees are from our own questionnaire; voting figures for the industrial workers from Olof Petersson and Bo Särlvik, "Valet 1973," *Allmänna valen 1973, del 3* (Swedish Official Statistics); statistics for collective affiliation from *Utveckling av organisation och verksamhet. Rapport från arbetsgruppen i organisationsfrågor* (Twenty-sixth Congress of the Social Democratic Party, 1975), (Stockholm: Tiden, 1975), p. 28. For the collectively affiliated locals information provided by the secretariat of the Social Democratic Party, where Björn Wall has been especially helpful. The collectively affiliated locals were registered by party district. Wall emphasizes that the figures are not exact; they may vary somewhat in either direction without altering the general picture.

a. The Musicians' and Seamen's unions as well as a few locals belonging to the Union of Insurance Employees have been excluded.

1,738 locals studied (out of a total of 1,952 in 1973) more than 97 percent had a Social Democratic governing committee. Only a handful of locals have a completely Communist leadership. A further definition of categories is necessary in order to be able to detect any variation whatever in this variable. In addition to the dominant group with an exclusively Social Democratic governing committee, there exists a category of locals that have at least one Communist committee member or representative or factional election with a Communist slate, and a small percentage of the locals belong to this category. A third category is constituted by locals with at least one non-socialist committee member or representative or factional election with a non-socialist slate; only a few tenths of one percent belong in this category. A fourth, if possible even smaller, category is marked by leadership described as "politically independent."

Table 2.7 also shows the voting of the industrial workers in the parliamentary elections of 1970. Here, too, the Social Democrats lead the list with 63 percent of the vote. They nevertheless fail to achieve the same position of total dominance among the rank and file as they do in the local governing committees. By comparing the statistics at these two levels—union leaders and ordinary workers—it is possible to discern a purposefully organized and determined elite in the Social Democratic Party, an elite directed toward winning and keeping practically all the top positions within the trade union movement. Thus, industrial workers with Communist sympathies, and to an even greater degree those with non-socialist sympathies, are very much underrepresented on the local governing committees.

Table 2.7 also includes data on the much debated collective affiliation (15) of trade union locals with the Social Democratic Party. Forty percent of the union locals fall into this category. If the question is reversed to ask what percentage of the Social Democratic membership is collectively affiliated with the party, the figure rises to 73 percent as of July 1, 1974! This figure is so high that the whole character of the Social Democratic Party as a mass party would be drastically altered if it, like the other political parties, had only individual affiliation.

Other parties consider collective affiliation of union locals with the Social Democratic Party a clear encroachment on freedom of opinion and a disgrace to Swedish democracy. Tens, possibly hundreds, of thousands of people are registered as members of the Social Democratic Party, in many cases against their knowledge or will. Collective affiliation has been constantly attacked in political campaigns and parliamentary debates during the 1960s and 1970s. During the recent large-scale constitutional reform, the Riksdag declared itself opposed in principle to collective affiliation, although a law to forbid this form of affiliation was rejected. By a vote of 167 to 143, the Riksdag approved the dissenting opinion of the constitutional committee in a clear unambiguous declaration:

> The right of the individual freely to choose a political party is fundamental to democracy. The committee, for reasons of principle, is therefore not able to accept the collective affiliation of individuals with a political party. The right of the individual to make a disclaimer in no way alters our view in this question of fundamental democratic importance. The present situation should be corrected, not through legislation, but through measures undertaken by the parties themselves. It is the hope of this committee that by turning public opinion against collective affiliation it will be possible to persuade the parties themselves to put an end to

this practice, so that only those persons who individually seek membership in a party are registered as members.

Following that declaration the Riksdag has annually renewed its con-
demnation of collective affiliation.[18]

Meanwhile, the Social Democrats maintain that the right of disclaimer
that the Riksdag finds unacceptable is a sufficient guarantee of democratic rights. When the Conservative leader Bohman brought up the
question of the Riksdag's declaration against collective affiliation during
the campaign of 1973, Minister of Finance Sträng said:

> There does exist, which Bohman does not mention, full right of dis-
> claimer. Anyone may get up and declare: "I don't like it. I don't want to
> belong. I disclaim party membership." Then he does not have to pay.
> Then Bohman says: "Isn't it embarrassing to have to get up and say: I am
> not a Social Democrat?" If you are of a different opinion, shouldn't you
> have enough courage to declare that "I am not a Social Democrat." He
> doesn't have to say that he is a Conservative—an exceptional case, but
> they do exist—or if he is a Liberal, if he belongs to the Farmer's Party, or
> the Center Party as they are called nowadays, or if he is a Communist. No
> one asks that of him. All he has to do is to say: "I don't want my money to
> go to the Social Democratic Party."[19]

It is not the task here to judge this and similar statements made by Social Democratic authorities. The object of political science is to weigh
ideological statements against political reality and to determine to what
extent they are valid. This study thus places great emphasis on analyzing
to what extent those not in sympathy with the Social Democrats, but yet
collectively affiliated, actually take advantage of their right of disclaimer. For if these people have been affiliated against their convictions
with a certain party with a certain view of society, it would seem indisputable that this is in violation of the rule of minority rights. In this connection, how common is harassment (14) of the fellow worker outside the
union movement by members and union leaders, and what form does it
take?

It is important for the trade union movement, as well as for other organizations founded on democratic ideals, to build and strengthen support
for union ideology (26). The leadership must win full acceptance among
the membership of certain basic ideas in the economic and political program of the movement—first and foremost a wage policy of solidarity.
The most effective tool by far in this ideological schooling effort is the
extensive study-activity (4) program of the union movement. The old
elementary school system did nothing to educate many of the leaders of
the popular movements. People's high schools and educational associa-

tions were founded for this purpose. In 1929, LO founded its first college, affiliated with the Brunnsvik People's High School; in 1953 the second, Runö College, was opened, and in 1074 the third, Hasseludden, outside Stockholm. There are also many different kinds of union-run study activity. First, the large number of study circles should be mentioned. Groups meet once or twice a week to study subjects often directly related to the job situations of the participants. During the winter of 1970–71, 87,000 persons, constituting 5 percent of the LO membership, participated in these groups. There are also the Fackliga centralorganisationerna [FCO, Local Trade Councils], the mission of which is to recruit new members, to disseminate information, and to conduct weekend courses. In addition, there are courses arranged by individual unions at the colleges or other study centers, as well as courses conducted there by LO. The latter courses are generally quite advanced and treat specific areas of union interest, such as job safety and industrial democracy. This type of course lasts anywhere from one week to three months.[20]

The key terms in analyzing the governance of the Swedish trade union movement are thus centralization and solidarity. Through centralization the movement has gradually been able to increase its power and realize its programs. An attempt has been made to strengthen the union ideology of solidarity through far-reaching, institutionalized cooperation between different workers' groups.

It is also necessary to focus upon a third set of conceptions relating to the governance of the Swedish trade union movement. These concern union apathy. From the very beginning there have been those who argued that the average member is not as interested in the struggle of labor as the militant leadership maintains. The low meeting attendance rate (2) in many locals is viewed as an indisputable expression of union apathy. This lack of interest among the membership is supposedly also demonstrated by infrequent discussion of union matters (3) with members of section or local committees and by the infrequent reading of the union periodical (5). Membership knowledge of union matters (9) is also questioned by those who point to union apathy, as is the sense of solidarity (13) with the movement in general. Conformism or a sense of compulsion is thought to be a more common reason for union membership than a sense of solidarity.

The foremost reason for union apathy is often said to be that the workers in today's affluent society, objectively speaking, have less reason to protest against their living conditions than they did before; the workers are reasonably satisfied, and devote their free time to activities other than the movement. Whether such a change in attitude actually has taken place can be shown at least indirectly by an analysis of the relationship between union democracy and the average length of membership (36) in the movement from the initial affiliation of a worker, including a possible change of local or union. Long-standing members might personally have experienced poverty and the early fight against it by the union movement, and might therefore feel a strong sense of union solidarity, whereas members who joined more recently might take affluence for granted and find union activity less important. Is union democracy more highly developed in unions with a greater average length of membership, or is there no such correlation?

Definite statements are often made concerning the effects of the development of society on union apathy. The development of sociotechnical conditions (33) at the place of work are mentioned as a contributing factor. On the one hand, an increasingly advanced technology is making industrial work physically less demanding, which ought to mean more energy left over for union issues. On the other hand, the new technology carries with it conditions unfavorable to engagement in union issues: the old work teams, the natural base units of the labor struggle, are broken up and replaced by the monotony of the conveyor belt, the isolation of ear protectors in noisy surroundings, or the cut-off feeling of the individual worker in a one-man–one-machine unit. Table 2.8 shows a number of indications of how sociotechnical conditions at the place of work vary from one union to another.

Another important factor contributing to union apathy is the increased mobility (34) within the country. The rapid structural changes in Swedish economic life, further hastened during the last fifteen years, have meant a new set of premises for union, as well as for Social Democratic Party, activity. In a mobile society people leave their old communities and their traditional contacts with the institutions of the workers' movement. The movement no longer has the same grip on the workers in the densely populated areas as it had in the old iron works and sawmills. This increased mobility and the inability of the workers' movement to inspire as strong a loyalty in society today as it did in the poor, class-ridden Sweden of an earlier period have been described as the greatest threats to the movement.

The people at the iron works and sawmills spent their free time within the framework of the workers' movement. The big events were the annual parties of the union and of the Cooperative Movement. All year round, entertainment consisted of the meetings and parties of the Party, the Women's Club, the Women's Guild, SSU (the Young Socialists), ABF (the Adult Education Program), and the labor union. But the influence of the

Table 2.8. Sociotechnical Conditions (by union).

Union	Heavy or Light Work[a]	Members Affected (percentage) by Certain Health Risks at Place of Work, 1968 (member survey)[b]					
		Load	Noise	Draft	Temperature	Rash	Dust
Building Maintenance Workers	L						
Building Workers	H	+70[c]	−35	+61	+31	+40	+33
Chimney Sweeps	L						
Electricians	L						
Factory Workers	H	−45	+53	+45	+31	+29	+22
Food Workers	H	−46	+44	+42	+38	+28	−3
Forest Workers	H						
Garment (leather) Workers	L	−32	−33	−25	−17	+33	−4
Garment (textiles) Workers	L	−39	+44	−28	+36	−23	+28
Graphic Industry Workers	H	(+)[d]	(+60)[d]	(40)[d]	(+50)[d]		(+)[d]
Hairdressers	L						
Hotel and Restaurant Workers	L						
Metal Workers	H	+53	+62	+42	+32	−20	−9
Miners	H	+61	+74	+54	−23	+28	+48
Municipal Workers	L	+59	−13	−19	−13	+44	−11
Painters	H	+65	−19	+59	−15	+78	+20
Pulp and Paper Workers	H	−40	+60	+49	+49	−19	−7
Sheet Metal Workers	H						
State Employees	L						
Transport Workers	H	−47	−29	−38	−17	−15	−10
Commercial Employees	L	−35	−10	−38	−23	−14	−2
Social Insurance Employees	L						
Wood Industry Workers	H	−45	+58	+53	+35	−25	−11
LO Average		51	41	40	29	25	14

a. The unions were classified by LO officials after a survey among the membership providing statistical material on accident rates, stress of chemical or technical nature, and ergonomic conditions.
b. Erik Bolinder, Egon Magnusson, and Lars Nyrén, *Risker i jobbet: LO enkäten* (Stockholm: Prisma, 1970).
c. Plus (+) or minus (−) indicates that the frequency of trouble is higher and lower respectively than the LO average.
d. Nicefor Czehowski and Egon Magnusson, *Risker i jobbet: Truckeri* (Stockholm: Prisma, 1970).

movement did not stop there. The organizations outside the movement, too, were drawn into its sphere. The membership and the leadership were the same. It was difficult to say where the movement began and ended . . . Today, the variety of tempting options for leisure time activities is, if possible, even greater, but also more commercialized—and de-politicized. In today's surroundings mobility and uncertainty have become part of life. Any group or individual affects only certain limited aspects of one's life. One owes allegiance to no one; one is freed from loyalties."[21]

How mobility varies from one union to another is shown in table 2.9. In addition to the extremely high figure for the Seamen (more than four-fifths of its membership is replaced annually), a high degree of mobility is found among the Hotel and Restaurant Workers, the Building Mainte-

Table 2.9. Union Mobility, 1974 (percentage).

Union	New Members	Memberships Discontinued
Agricultural Workers	16.3	20.1
Building Maintenance Workers	28.8	28.2
Building Workers	5.3	7.8
Chimney Sweeps	11.6	15.8
Electricians	7.0	5.7
Factory Workers	22.1	17.6
Food Workers	17.6	16.5
Forest Workers	8.9	14.0
Garment Workers	19.6	20.4
Graphic Industry Workers	11.1	9.2
Hairdressers	22.9	32.5
Hotel and Restaurant Workers	34.4	33.8
Metal Workers	17.7	10.5
Miners	17.7	15.4
Municipal Workers	14.1	8.0
Musicians	24.8	30.1
Painters	4.7	8.2
Pulp and Paper Workers	15.4	12.4
Seamen	81.8	81.2
Sheet Metal Workers	—	—
State Employees	6.9	5.7
Transport Workers	20.5	13.9
Commercial Employees	16.9	16.9
Social Insurance Employees	12.4	7.8
Wood Industry Workers	15.5	14.6
LO total	15.5	12.4

Source: *LO Statistics,* 1974 (Stockholm, 1974).

nance Workers, the Musicians, and the Hairdressers. Among unions with a low degree of mobility are Building Workers, Painters, and State Employees.

Democracy can be correlated to sex (35) distribution in the unions. Women have always, for various reasons which we need not go into here, been less active than men when it comes to union-related or political matters. The general development of society has brought more and more women into the labor market and membership in LO (see table 2.10); the distribution of women among the different unions is indicated in table 2.11. The successful recruiting of women by the unions has in all likelihood meant a slowdown of membership activity as the proportion of women has increased—a growth problem commonly found in organizations gradually moving from an elite nucleus toward a more apathetic periphery.

In both the trade union movement and other democratic organizations, membership apathy tends to weaken the strength of the movement. The Swedish unions have therefore delegated considerable resources to a program of ideological training—too vigorous in the view of some—the purpose of which is the activation of the rank and file and the subsequent revitalization of union democracy. The leadership realized early that the struggle against the employers could be won only through cooperation among various workers' groups. Through extensive centralization and creation of a professional, highly competent, expert bureaucracy, LO has become the most powerful interest group in Sweden. Cooperation also served to strengthen the ideology of solidarity that is deeply rooted in socialism. To raise the workers' wages at the expense

Table 2.10. Women Members of LO, 1900–1974.

Year	Number	Percentage
1900	1,029	2.4
1910	5,715	6.7
1920	32,787	11.7
1930	57,807	10.4
1940	157,904	16.3
1950	240,423	18.8
1960	334,840	22.5
1970	480,532	28.6
1974	613,157	32.9

Source: *LO Statistics*, 1974 (Stockholm, 1974), p. 34.

Table 2.11. Women Members of National Unions, 1974.

Union	Number	Percentage of Total
Agricultural Workers	1,646	13.9
Building Maintenance Workers	19,016	56.5
Building Workers	2,731	1.7
Chimney Sweeps	1	0.0
Electricians	30	0.1
Factory Workers	28,331	28.3
Food Workers	21,329	39.6
Forest Workers	609	2.5
Garment Workers	37,994	67.3
Graphic Industry Workers	9,418	24.2
Hairdressers	3,511	88.1
Hotel and Restaurant Workers	21,467	80.2
Metal Workers	68,478	15.4
Miners	883	6.5
Municipal Workers	229,366	74.2
Musicians	914	10.1
Painters	30	0.1
Pulp and Paper Workers	7,037	14.2
Seamen	3,166	20.8
Sheet Metal Workers	1	0.0
State Employees	40,329	23.1
Transport Workers	4,588	9.1
Commercial Employees	93,172	69.9
Social Insurance Employees	10,883	63.9
Wood Industry Workers	8,227	10.3
Total	613,157	32.9

Source: *LO Statistics*, 1974 (Stockholm, 1974), p. 37.

of the capitalists was no longer a sufficient goal. Instead, the main characteristic of the Swedish trade union movement was its deep commitment to a more equitable and equal distribution of wages among the different working groups.

Defining the Democratic Model

There are two separate points of departure for this study. First, there is the guiding democratic theory discussed in the first chapter. Second, in order to interpret the concrete phenomena associated with trade union government within the conceptual framework of interactive democracy,

it is necessary to specify the model of democracy and to make it relevant
to the governance of the Swedish trade union movement. The normative
postulate of the model of interactive democracy is public spirit. The
wage policy of solidarity represents the empirical application of this
postulate. In the shaping of the program of the labor movement, the role
played by a wage policy of solidarity is decisive. Does a wage policy of
solidarity really aim at furthering the development of public spirit in the
individual member, and does such a wage policy constitute the primary
objective of union democracy?

In order to decide questions of a similar interpretative nature political
scientists commonly resort to genetic idea analysis, by which the suc-
cessive development of an ideology under the influence of different expe-
riences and impulses is traced through the study of program statements,
debates, decisions, and actions taken. However, as other researchers have
pointed out, the source situation is unusual. In the LO material—mo-
tions, minutes, rules, programs, and so forth—solidarity is assumed to be
a desirable goal, which should be pursued, but it is never questioned, and
to do so at all would be unseemly. Solidarity with the economically disadvantaged is expressed in such phrases as "self-evident," "natural," "an
expression of socialist values," "part of the historic task of the workers'
movement," and so forth. The LO material is dominated by a sophisti-
cated statistical account and a string of economic analyses of wage development. Because the wage policy of solidarity has been shaped by
economists and not by political scientists, the economic results of this
policy have been effected, even though there is a real lack of knowledge
of consensus of opinion and authority in the LO ranks. It may be possible
to claim that the meagerness of the debate, which displays both a lack of
interest in political value questions and a preoccupation with economic
and technical solutions, is a typically Swedish phenomenon. In the larger
European countries to the south, the debate is more philosophical and
rhetorical, centering on solidarity and equality *contra* the principle of
wages by performance. Because of Nordic reticence on this aspect, it is
easy to conclude, erroneously, that ideologies are less important to the
Swedes than to others. Actually the opposite is true: there is probably no
labor movement in the world that is more successful than the Swedish in
achieving an ideologically motivated narrowing of the wage spread.
However, the available sources do not reveal the motivations of the
unions in pursuing this policy of equalization.[22]

Against this background, how should the efforts by unions to put into
practice a wage policy of solidarity be interpreted in terms of union democracy? The educating of the individual member to active and com-

mitted support for the idea of economic solidarity among different membership groups is a goal that, even if the unarticulated but unambiguous LO material does not actually link it to the name of John Stuart Mill, is best represented by the normative idea of public spirit and the democratic model of interactive democracy. Rousseau's model of political equality cannot be applied in this case, for solidarity requires a far-reaching centralization; solidarity with a weak government would be a very inconsistent model, an extremely inefficient organization. Weber's model is closer to the Swedish union movement, but in the trade union research inspired by his theories, there is no trace of democratic schooling to solidarity. The Leninist model, which prescribes that the program of the unions be subordinate to the Party leadership in the fight against capitalism, is unable to include a wage policy of solidarity. From a Leninist point of view, what is such a policy but a plea for a weakening of the class struggle against the most profitable industries, which then would not have to pay high wages? Schumpeter's more formal model of competition takes scant interest in the economic program of labor or a policy of wage solidarity. The same thing might be said of the likewise more formal representational model. However, the model of interactive democracy takes as its very departure point a concept closely related to a wage policy of solidarity: to increase the public spirit of the individual member through interaction with the leadership in such a way that he also develops a sense of responsibility and solidarity with other, less favored groups.

Figure 2.3 defines and interprets the general democratic values from figure 1.1 in terms of union-related phenomena, and table 2.12 contains the comprehensive overview of these values also in terms of union-related phenomena. In further specifying functional values, "Activity" is the first value of the variable of opinion-formation. In figure 2.3 this is symbolized by *membership attendance rate* at meetings; in table 2.12 this is complemented by the frequency of *discussion of union matters* between members and officials, the extent of *study activity* and *reading of union periodical*, and the amount of time devoted by the leadership to *union-related work, discussion with members, study activity*, and *informational activity*.

"Competence" is the second value of the variable of opinion-formation. In figure 2.3, it is symbolized by membership *knowledge of union matters* and in table 2.12 is complemented by *leadership acquaintance with the members, understanding of the text of the agreement*, and *knowledge of membership opinion*.

"System orientation" constitutes the third value. In figure 2.3 this is

Table 2.12. Union-Related Phenomena.

	Phenomenon		
Value	Membership[a]	Leadership	Number[b]
Public spirit	Wage policy of solidarity (pl)	—	1
Opinion-formation			
Activity	Meeting attendance rate		2
	Discussion of union matters		3
	Study activity		4
	Reading of periodical		5
		Union-related work	6
		Discussion with members	7
		Study activity	4
		Provide information	8
Competence	Knowledge of union matters (p1)		9
		Acquaintance with members	10
		Understand agreement	11
		Know membership opinion (p1)	12
System orientation	Solidarity		13
	Harassment		14
	Collective affiliation (p1)		15
	System of representation		16
	Top officials		17
	Representatives (ombudsmen)		18
	Trust in local and section leaderships		19
		Idealism	20
		Collective affiliation	15
		Membership activity (pl)	21
		Top officials	17
Consensus-building			
Legitimacy	Union elections (p1)		22
Agreement of opinion	Bossism (p1)	Bossism (p1)	23
Demands	Union dissatisfaction (p1)		24
		"Neglected issues"	25
Schooling	Union ideology (p1)	Union ideology (p1)	26
		Conception of leadership	27
Decision–nondecision	Union as fighting organization (p1)	Union as fighting organization (p1)	28
Authority	Wildcat strikes (p1)		29

Table 2.12 (*continued*)

	Phenomenon		
Value	Membership[a]	Leadership	Number[b]
Independent variables			
Organizational structure			
including district			30
branch reform (pl)			31
Wages			32
Sociotechnical conditions			33
Mobility			34
Sex			35
Length of membership			36
Political party preferences			37

a. (pl) after a phenomenon indicates that more than one question will be used as a measure in the operationalization.

b. Numbers in this column refer to phenomena listed in the previous section.

shown as membership and leadership attitudes toward *collective affiliation*, complemented in table 2.12 by the extent of membership feeling of *solidarity* with the labor movement, awareness of *harassment* of those outside the unions, attitude toward the *system of representation, top officials and representatives*, degree of *trust in local and section leadership*, as well as the extent to which committee members are motivated by *idealism* in accepting office, their attitude toward *membership activity* and their attitude toward *top officials*.

The next variable is "consensus-building." The first value is "legitimacy," defined as certain requirements for *union elections*. The second, "agreement of opinion" between membership and leadership, is defined in an analysis as whether the talk of *bossism* within the labor movement is justified (this much discussed phenomenon has been selected to symbolize the definition of the consensus variable in figure 2.3). The third value consists of "demands," defined as the extent of membership *dissatisfaction* with wages, as well as whether there are *"neglected issues"* within the local, in the eyes of the committee members. The fourth value "schooling" is described as the attitudes held by the membership and the leadership toward *union ideology* and the *conception of leadership* by the committee members.

The variable "decision-nondecision" is analyzed as the extent to which the various locals function as *fighting organizations* according to the radical demand—organizations single-mindedly backing the expressed interests of the rank and file without regard for union coordination, state

Figure 2.3. Specification of the Interactive Democracy Model: Examples of Union-Related Phenomena. Numbers in parentheses refer to phenomena listed in the previous section.

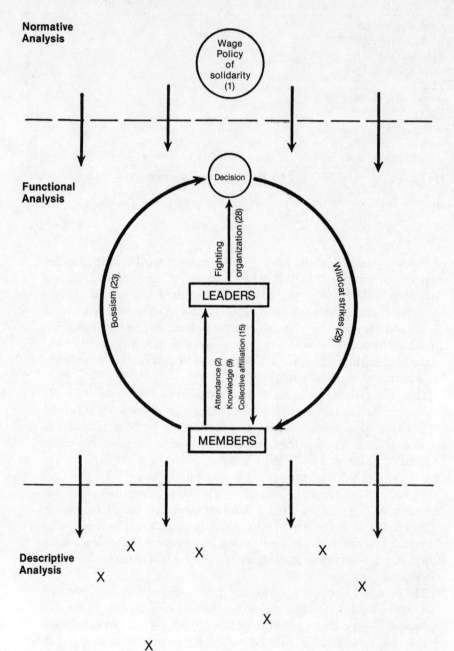

Figure 2.4. Independent and Dependent Variables of the Study.

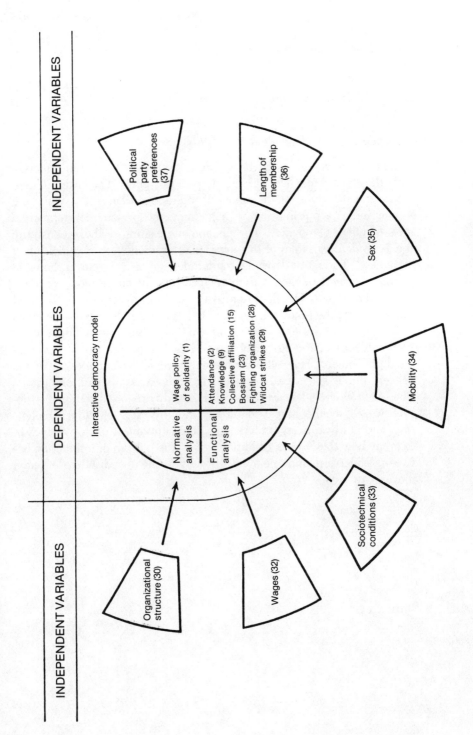

INDEPENDENT VARIABLES

DEPENDENT VARIABLES

INDEPENDENT VARIABLES

Political party preferences (37)

Length of membership (36)

Sex (35)

Mobility (34)

Sociotechnical conditions (33)

Wages (32)

Organizational structure (30)

Interactive democracy model

Normative analysis

Functional analysis

Wage policy of solidarity (1)

Attendance (2)
Knowledge (9)
Collective affiliation (15)
Bossism (23)
Fighting organization (28)
Wildcat strikes (29)

regulations, or counterproposals from the employer. This phenomenon is also included in figure 2.3.

Finally, the variable "authority" is defined as a study of *wildcat strikes* and is also found in figure 2.3.

Dependent and Independent Variables

Some phenomena enumerated in table 2.12 perform a different function from those that have been discussed up to this point. The latter all constitute specifications for the model of interactive democracy, while the former indicate possible factors explaining the present developmental level of union democracy. The phenomena examined above constitute the *dependent* variables of this inquiry, the remaining, the *independent* variables.[23] The set of dependent and independent variables is shown in figure 2.4. The dependent variables constitute the entire model of interactive democracy. The figure omits the level of descriptive analysis of the model. At the functional level, only a few examples have been given of how the four variables (opinion-formation, consensus-building, decision-nondecision, and authority) have been defined in terms of union-related phenomena. However, the normative level is complete in that the concept public spirit has been defined as the wage policy of solidarity.[24] The seven independent variables of this study are: organizational structure, wages, sociotechnical conditions, mobility, sex, length of membership, and political party preferences. The main object of this study is to examine how these seven conditions affect the pattern of interaction between leadership and membership within the Swedish trade union movement.

3

Members and Leaders: Agreement and Disagreement

In the course of sampling and fieldwork, it was necessary to narrow further the definition of the model of democracy in order to make it relevant to the governance of Swedish trade unions.

Sampling and Fieldwork

The *sample selection* and *fieldwork* of this inquiry[1] included the following levels of the trade union movement: (1) general membership; (2) section committees; (3) local executive committees; (4) central (national) level.[2] The fourth, "central," level consists of all members of the executive committees of the national trade unions as well as the General Council. The research is thus inclusive rather than based on a sample at this level.

In the case of levels one, two, and three it was necessary to be selective.[3] First, 1,738 of the 1,952 locals affiliated with LO in 1973 were considered. Both the Seamen's Union and the Musicians' Union were excluded from the outset, as well as certain locals within the Social Insurance Employees' Union. The Seamen's Union contains no locals corresponding to those of other unions with elected leadership, meetings, and so forth; it has only special representatives in the various port cities. Many of the members of the Musicians' Union are part-time musicians and are affiliated with other unions. In the Social Insurance Employees' Union part-time insurance agents have been excluded, because again many have double affiliations. Five nationwide locals with district managers within the Social Insurance Employees' Union have also been left out.

Extensive data for all 1,738 locals were gathered. With this background it was possible to stratify the locals according to certain variables. The task proved time consuming in the extreme because not all of the union offices possessed registers with the information required. When the list finally was complete, it contained information on the following stratification variables for the 1,738 union locals: (1) organizational structure; (2) wages; (3) sociotechnical conditions; (4) mobility; (5) sex; (6) length of membership; and (7) political party preferences. These stratification variables are identical to the independent variables previously presented (see figure 2.4).

Next it was necessary to provide a representative sample. Prompted by various considerations, the following sampling design was selected. During the first phase, 50 locals would be drawn. During the second, the individuals, members as well as officials, would be drawn. The first six independent variables presented no problem as to representativity. The 1,738 locals were relatively evenly distributed over these variable values. The extremely lopsided distribution of the locals within the political party preference variable, on the other hand, proved to have some consequences for the sampling.[4]

During the spring of 1974 the data for the independent variables, gathered through a special questionnaire that was sent to the officials of the 50 union locals, were checked and completed. Table 3.1 indicates the values that the independent variables assumed and the way that the 50 locals were distributed according to these values.

The organizational structure variable assumes three values: (1) "district branches with representational bodies"; (2) "district branches without representational bodies"; and (3) "smaller locals." Approximately the same number of district branches and smaller locals were found; among the district branches those with representational bodies predominate.

The wage variable, too, assumes three values: (1) "high wage," an hourly rate of no less than 18.00 Swedish crowns; (2) "medium wage," an hourly wage rate that ranges from 15.01 to 17.99 Swedish crowns; and (3) "low wage," an hourly wage rate of no more than 15.00 Swedish crowns.

In the case of the third variable, "sociotechnical conditions," the views expressed by the local union officials themselves in response to the questionnaire as to the nature and physical environment of the job were compared to the opinions of the central LO functionaries (table 2.8). In this way the three categories and their distribution indicated by the table were determined.

Mobility as a variable was determined by relating the membership turnover to the size of the local. There are three groups: (1) "low," a mobility rate of no more than 9.99 percent; (2) "medium," a mobility rate that varies from 10 to 19.99 percent; and (3) "high," a mobility rate of more than 20 percent. A fourth category, "immigrants," was established

Table 3.1. Independent Stratification Variables in Fifty Locals by Variable Value.

Independent Stratification Variable	Number of Locals
Organizational structure	
District branches with representational bodies	15
District branches without representational bodies	9
Smaller locals	26
Total	50
Wages	
High	15
Medium	19
Low	16
Total	50
Sociotechnical conditions	
Light work	13
Medium	19
Heavy	18
Total	50
Mobility	
Low	10
Medium	15
High	17
High; many immigrants	8
Total	50
Sex (% male)	
90–100	24
75–89	12
0–74	14
Total	50
Length of membership	
Short	15
Medium	24
Long	11
Total	50
Political party preferences	
Social Democratic	40
Communist	10
Total	50

for locals with a membership of at least 9 percent immigrants. The locals in this fourth category show a high rate of mobility.

The values and distributions of the variable "sex" are: (1) locals with a male membership between 90 and 100 percent; (2) those with a male membership between 75 and 89 percent; and (3) those with a male membership below 75 percent.

The variable "length of membership" has the following limits: (1) "short," an average length of membership not exceeding 14.99 years; (2) "medium," an average length of membership that varies between 15.00 and 19.99 years; and (3) "long," an average length of membership of more than 20 years.

The political party preference variable, finally, is limited to two values: (1) "Social Democratic" locals; and (2) "Communist" locals. Only the party preferences expressed by the local committee members were included—a study of the party preferences of the rank and file would have been a task of gigantic dimensions.[5] The position of the Social Democratic Party is virtually unchallenged in this area. More than 97 percent of the original 1,738 locals had Social Democratic committees, while locals the committees of which showed a preference for the non-socialist parties or were politically uncommitted accounted for less than 1 percent. It should be noted that the term "Communist committee" was defined very loosely, with no insistence on a completely Communist steering committee, or even a Communist majority. A local was said to be Communist if it had (1) at least one Communist committee member; (2) a Communist representative; or (3) factional elections with a Communist program. The study of political party preferences may contain some minor errors, and the actual number of Communist locals may be somewhat larger than what was found.

In order to be able to include Communist locals in our sample at all, we decided beforehand to set aside 10 of the 50 sample locals for Communist locals. Ten Communist union locals were drawn on a nonstatistical basis. Those that were most Communist—that is, had the greatest number of Communists on the steering committees and so forth—were selected. From the remaining 1,700 locals in the population, 40 were drawn by a selection system based on equal probability: the probability being $40:1,700 = 0.02352941$. None of the small number of non-socialist or "politically uncommitted" locals was drawn in the sample of 40. All were Social Democratic.

The 10 Communist and the 40 Social Democratic locals were weighted according to the probability of selection. Another prerequisite of material subjected to quantitative analysis is what is commonly referred to as multicollinearity, which means that the independent variables must not be too highly correlated. If the correlation between two independent variables is perfect or very close, it becomes impossible to decide which one of them is the originator of the phenomenon to be explained. In this material, for example, it might be expected that union locals with low wages would also contain a higher percentage of women. If the correlation coefficient between wages and sex had approached 1, difficulties would have been encountered, even though it might have been possible to devise ways to circumvent them.[6] A simple correlative estimate (see table 3.2) showed the multicollinearity not to be too high. The highest coefficient found in the matrix is −0.5734 between sociotechnical conditions and sex: locals in occupations with heavy work contain fewer women. The correlation at this level is, if not perfect, at least acceptable. The second highest coefficient 0.5150 is found between wages and sex: locals with a higher proportion of women tend to have lower wages. The third highest coefficient −0.4866 occurs between mobility and length of membership: the annual turnover is lower in locals with a longer average time of union affiliation. The fourth highest coefficient −0.4573 is found between wages and political party preferences, a not unknown, but nevertheless in no way self-evident correlation. A closer look at the correlative calculations reveals that wages tend to be higher in Communist locals. Beyond that, the correlative values of the matrix decrease.

Before continuing the explanation of the selection process, it might be interesting to view the distribution of the 50 locals from two other dimensions, even if these will not later be used as independent analytical variables: (1) the geographic distribution of the locals and (2) their distribution by national union. The geographic distribution is shown in figure 3.1 (to make positive identification more difficult, the locals have been

Table 3.2. Multicollinearity: Correlation among Independent Variables Expressed as Correlation Coefficients (O = Organizational structure; W = Wages; ST = Sociotechnical conditions; M = Mobility; S = Sex; Me = Length of membership; P = Political party preference).

	O	W	ST	M	S	Me	P
O	1.0000						
W	−0.0353	1.0000					
ST	−0.1778	−0.2310	1.0000				
M	−0.2096	0.3754	−0.0599	1.0000			
S	−0.1020	0.5150	−0.5734	0.3018	1.0000		
Me	0.2821	−0.3517	0.1930	−0.4866	−0.3881	1.0000	
P	−0.3529	−0.4573	0.2561	−0.3353	−0.2946	0.0558	1.0000

66

Governing Trade Unions in Sweden

Figure 3.1. Geographic Distribution of the Fifty Locals Sampled.

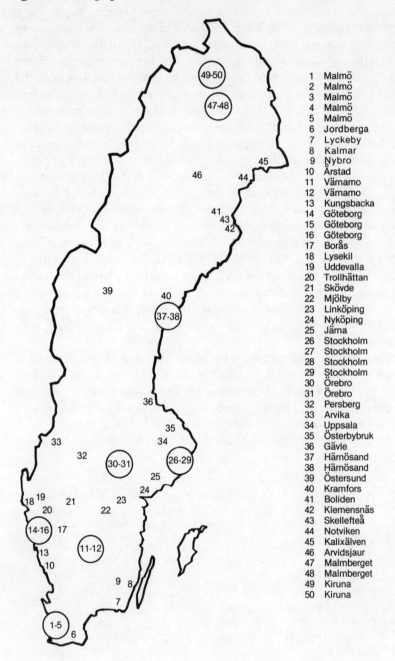

1	Malmö
2	Malmö
3	Malmö
4	Malmö
5	Malmö
6	Jordberga
7	Lyckeby
8	Kalmar
9	Nybro
10	Årstad
11	Värnamo
12	Värnamo
13	Kungsbacka
14	Göteborg
15	Göteborg
16	Göteborg
17	Borås
18	Lysekil
19	Uddevalla
20	Trollhättan
21	Skövde
22	Mjölby
23	Linköping
24	Nyköping
25	Järna
26	Stockholm
27	Stockholm
28	Stockholm
29	Stockholm
30	Örebro
31	Örebro
32	Persberg
33	Arvika
34	Uppsala
35	Österbybruk
36	Gävle
37	Härnösand
38	Härnösand
39	Östersund
40	Kramfors
41	Boliden
42	Klemensnäs
43	Skellefteå
44	Notviken
45	Kalixälven
46	Arvidsjaur
47	Malmberget
48	Malmberget
49	Kiruna
50	Kiruna

numbered differently here from their numeration elsewhere and arranged consecutively from south to north). In this figure an even distribution of locals is found over the country; several locals are concentrated in and around the larger cities and a few other localities.

The distribution by union of the sample locals is indicated in table 3.3. Before the sampling began, the total number of locals was arranged by national unions, which increased the probability that every union would find itself represented in the sample. This proved to be the case (with the above-mentioned exceptions of the Musicians' and Seamen's unions). Unions with a large number of locals, such as the State Employees, Metal Workers, and Agricultural Workers, are represented by several locals; others with fewer locals are represented by one only. The total number of locals affiliated with a union, not their individual size, was the deciding factor determining the distribution of the sample locals by union.

Table 3.3. Sample Locals by Union.

Union	Number of Locals
Agricultural Workers	5
Building Maintenance Workers	1
Building Workers	3
Chimney Sweeps	1
Electricians	2
Factory Workers	2
Food Workers	1
Forest Workers	2
Garment Workers	1
Graphic Industry Workers	3
Hairdressers	1
Hotel and Restaurant Workers	1
Metal Workers	6
Miners	4
Municipal Workers	2
Painters	2
Pulp and Paper Workers	2
Sheet Metal Workers	1
State Employees	6
Transport Workers	1
Commercial Employees	1
Social Insurance Employees	1
Wood Industry Workers	1
Total	50

By examining 50 locals it is possible to determine the interaction between the rank and file and their leaders. The locals, not the individual
members, are the chief protagonists of this book, and it is the governance
of the unions that is investigated. "Membership opinion" on a given issue
will be arrived at by weighting the individual responses proportionately
to the size of the local because an equal number of members have been
drawn from each local regardless of size.

The second step of the sampling process was the selection of the individual members, section committee members, and local executive committee members. At the membership level a sample of 50 members was
drawn from each of the 50 locals—provided they contained at least that
number; if not, the total membership was included. This resulted in a
sample of 2,294 members. From each of the 24 union locals in the sample
that have sections, all of the section committee members were drawn, or
a sample of 15, if there were more. This resulted in a total of 304 individuals at the section committee level. All members of the steering committees of the union locals were included, a total of 354. As mentioned
previously, no drawing was needed at the fourth, central, level. Everyone on the committees of the national unions, as well as the General
Council, was included, which gave a group of 272 individuals. All individuals were sent a questionnaire.

In order to compose the questionnaire a series of test interviews was
conducted in the fall of 1973 and spring of 1974. In order to take into account the differences in organizational structure and nomenclature
among the individual unions, it was necessary to print the questionnaire
in several versions, including one in Finnish (the questionnaires are re-
printed in the Code Book). A letter of recommendation from LO chairman Gunnar Nilsson was enclosed with the questionnaire.

The questionnaire was sent out to the general membership on May 3,
1974. The response rate is shown in figure 3.2.[7] As of May 21 somewhat
less than half of the members had responded, and the first reminder was
sent out. The number of responses had risen to 63 percent by June 6.
Then a second reminder was mailed, and it included a new form plus a
letter in English, German, French, Greek, and Serbo-Croatian, instruct-
ing those who spoke no Swedish to return the letter and indicate their
nationality. The vacation period yielded poor results. Between July 5,
when 74 percent of the total had responded, and August 7 only 18 additional replies were received. A third reminder was sent on August 22
with limited success. Some other method was needed.

On September 4 a series of telephone interviews with those who had
not previously responded was begun. In this way, an additional 350 re-

Figure 3.2. Fieldwork at the Membership Level (R = reminder; NRS = nonrespondent sample; tel. = telephoned reminder).

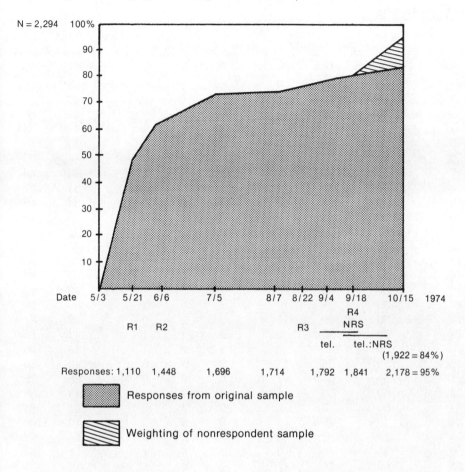

Responses from original sample

Weighting of nonrespondent sample

plies from members were received over a period of a few weeks. On September 18 a fourth reminder was mailed to certain special groups including, among others, all the members drawn from three locals with a below-average response rate.

On the same day an analysis of the nonrespondents was initiated. Of the 435 members who had not replied, every fifth was drawn, and a new questionnaire sent; 33 replied. The nonrespondent sample was then approached through telephone interviews. In this way an additional 31 replies were received. Of the original 87 in the nonrespondent sample, 64 were thus accounted for. In the statistical preparation, the individuals in

Table 3.4. Response Frequency: Membership Level by Local (N = Sample; Q = Response through questionnaire, including four reminders; T = Response through telephone interviews)

Local	Original Sample			Nonrespondent Sample			Frequency	
	N	Q	T	N	Q	T	Absolute Number	Percentage
1	50	33	9	2	1	0	43	86
2	24	16	0	2	0	0	16	67
3	50	32	6	2	2	0	40	80
4	50	33	9	2	1	1	44	88
5	50	32	9	2	1	1	43	86
6	50	35	10	1	0	1	46	92
7	50	35	7	2	1	1	44	88
8	50	33	7	2	1	0	41	82
9	50	31	3	3	0	0	34	68
10	50	28	7	3	2	1	38	76
11	37	24	7	1	0	1	32	87
12	50	28	11	2	1	0	40	80
13	50	34	8	2	1	1	44	88
14	50	31	9	2	0	1	41	82
15	50	26	9	3	0	1	36	72
16	50	28	10	2	0	1	39	78
17	50	29	11	2	2	0	42	84
18	50	33	9	2	1	1	44	88
19	50	36	8	1	0	1	45	90
20	50	28	11	2	1	0	40	80
21	50	31	7	2	0	0	38	76
22	50	36	6	2	1	1	44	88
23	50	37	5	2	2	0	44	88
24	10	10	0	0	0	0	10	100
25	13	12	0	0	0	0	12	92
26	15	10	0	1	0	1	11	73
27	50	26	12	2	0	1	39	78
28	39	26	6	1	0	1	33	85
29	50	32	4	3	2	0	38	76
30	50	38	8	1	0	1	47	94
31	50	29	11	2	2	0	42	84
32	50	39	6	1	0	1	46	92
33	50	31	9	2	1	1	42	84
34	50	35	7	2	1	1	44	88
35	50	28	8	3	1	1	38	76
36	50	34	9	1	1	0	44	88
37	50	36	5	2	0	2	43	86
38	50	33	7	2	2	0	42	84
39	6	5	0	0	0	0	5	83

Table 3.4 (*continued*)

Local	Original Sample			Nonrespondent Sample			Frequency	
							Absolute Number	Percentage
	N	Q	T	N	Q	T		
40	50	29	9	2	1	0	39	78
41	50	37	5	2	2	0	44	88
42	50	34	9	1	0	1	44	88
43	50	37	4	2	0	2	43	86
44	50	28	10	2	0	1	39	76
45	50	40	7	1	0	1	48	96
46	50	27	6	3	0	0	33	66
47	50	40	5	1	1	0	46	92
48	50	36	8	1	1	0	45	90
49	50	34	7	2	0	2	43	86
50	50	33	10	1	0	1	44	88
Total	2,294	1,508	350	87	33	31	1,922	84

the nonrespondent sample were given the weight of five, because every fifth had been drawn, while those in the original sample had the weight of one.[8] The fieldwork at the membership level was concluded on October 15, 1974. A weighted response frequency of 95 percent had been achieved, corresponding to 2,178 of the original 2,294 members drawn.

However, it is not enough to make a general statement concerning the response rate. Several analyses treat each local separately, and it was therefore necessary to make certain that the response frequency was sufficiently high for each of the 50 locals. The result is shown in table 3.4. The 50 locals are listed separately in order. The second column shows that in the majority of cases a full 50 members were drawn; only seven locals show less than 50 members, which in each case represents the entire membership. The next column indicates the number of responses to the questionnaire, including some that required as many as four reminders. The result of the telephone interviews within the original sample is listed next. The first column in the nonrespondent analysis indicates the distribution of the 87 individuals in this sample among the various locals. The next two columns show the responses from questionnaires and telephone interviews, respectively. Finally, the response frequency in absolute numbers and percentages is listed.

Two factors combined to ensure a sufficiently high response frequency in each individual local. First, the fourth reminder was directed specifically to locals with a low response frequency. Second, the locals with a low response frequency had more members represented in the nonrespondent sample than those with a high response frequency.

The fieldwork at the membership level proved to be especially complicated compared to the other levels with their significantly smaller samples. The questionnaire to the section and local committee members was sent out at the same time as the membership questionnaires on May 3, with reminders on May 21 and June 6. On August 7, after the vacation period had ended, there had been a response frequency of 76 percent among the section committees and 82 percent among the union local committees (at this date the rank and file response was 75 percent). A third reminder yielded a poor result. Instead of telephone interviews, telephoned reminders and persuasive arguments in favor of a response were used. Just as was the case at the membership level, a fourth reminder was sent to some committees with especially low response rates. Twenty committee members responded to this. A nonrespondent analysis was not considered necessary at these levels. The final tally on October 25 showed a response frequency of 83 percent for section committee members, and 94 percent for members of the steering committees of the union locals. These figures, too, have been broken down by individual local, as shown in tables 3.5 and 3.6. N represents the total number of individuals on the committees, unless the section committee includes more than 15, where the sample is limited to that number.

The fieldwork at the central level was started somewhat later; the questionnaire was sent out on August 29. The replies came back at a satisfactory rate, in a steady trickle, and after two reminders the fieldwork was concluded on November 22 with a final response rate for the central level of 93 percent (see table 3.7). All the material was then coded and processed by the computers at Uppsala Datacentral.[9]

Results

The results were arranged by previously specified democratic values (summarized in table 2.12): (1) public spirit; (2) activity; (3) competence; (4) system orientation; (5) legitimacy; (6) agreement of opinion; (7) demands; (8) schooling; (9) decision and nondecision; (10) authority; and (11) analysis of district branch reform.

Public Spirit

The development of public spirit constitutes the normative postulate for the model of interactive democracy. In this study it has been specified as

Table 3.5. Response Frequency: Section Committee Level (based on twenty-four locals with sections; N = Sample; R = Response, questionnaire including four written and one telephoned reminders).

Local	N	R	Percentage
1	15	14	93
3	15	11	73
4	15	11	73
5	9	7	78
6	15	12	80
10	7	7	100
14	15	13	87
16	15	13	87
17	15	12	80
20	15	11	73
21	9	8	89
22	15	13	87
23	15	11	73
29	10	9	90
30	15	13	87
31	6	6	100
32	15	11	73
36	13	13	100
37	3	2	67
40	15	13	87
41	15	12	80
47	7	7	100
49	15	12	80
50	15	12	80
Total	304	253	83

encompassing a wage policy of solidarity (phenomenon 1). Three questions were asked to ascertain opinions at each of the four levels: members, section committee, local steering committee, and the central level (see table 3.8). The first operationalization consists of the question whether the respondent himself would be willing to forego a raise if this would benefit low-income earners belonging to another union. This question reflects the most important aspect of public spirit, for it indicates the individual's psychological willingness to contribute to the improved situation of another and not his concern for his own benefits. Less than half of the members answered the question in the affirmative; the figure is higher at the higher levels.

The two other questions indicate more of a position in principle toward the theory of a wage policy of solidarity. There was overwhelming

Table 3.6. Response Frequency: Local Committee Level by Local (N = Sample; R = Response, questionnaire including four written and one telephoned reminders).

Local	N	R	Percentage
1	7	7	100
2	4	4	100
3	9	9	100
4	11	11	100
5	7	7	100
6	9	9	100
7	7	5	71
8	5	5	100
9	4	4	100
10	7	7	100
11	7	7	100
12	6	6	100
13	7	6	86
14	15	13	87
15	7	6	86
16	9	8	89
17	9	8	89
18	5	5	100
19	9	8	89
20	12	10	83
21	7	7	100
22	11	11	100
23	7	6	86
24	3	3	100
25	4	3	75
26	4	3	75
27	4	4	100
28	5	5	100
29	7	7	100
30	9	8	89
31	9	8	89
32	9	7	78
33	5	5	100
34	7	7	100
35	5	5	100
36	7	6	86
37	9	9	100
38	7	7	100
39	4	4	100
40	9	9	100
41	7	7	100

Table 3.6 (*continued*)

Local	N	R	Percentage
42	3	3	100
43	8	8	100
44	5	5	100
45	6	6	100
46	7	6	86
47	7	7	100
48	7	7	100
49	9	9	100
50	7	7	100
Total	354	334	94

support at all levels for the notion that better-paid groups should support low-income groups, even if this means that their own demands must be set aside. The third question concerns the economic and political consequences of the wage policy. The wage policy of the last fifteen years has aimed at an increased structural rationalization of the economy—the theory being that only through greater efficiency, mobility, and flexibility can real economic equality be accomplished. This aspect of the wage policy of solidarity found less support among the rank and file, whereas at the higher levels there was considerable support for this theory.[10]

The objective of the interactive democracy model is the development of the public spirit of the individual member only, not that of the officials. Less than 5 out of every 10 members were prepared to forego a raise in favor of the low-wage earners; almost 8 out of 10 thought that those who are well paid should support the low-income workers; and 4 out of every 10 members were prepared to risk the closing of industries as a consequence of far-reaching wage demands. These are the figures that constitute the basis for the comparison of the realization of public spirit within different organizations.

The three higher levels have been included in order to investigate

Table 3.7. Response Frequency: Central Level (N = Total number; R = Response, questionnaire including two reminders).

N	R	Percentage
272	252	93

Table 3.8. Attitude toward a Wage Policy of Solidarity (N = Total number; M = Members; S = Section committee members; L = Local committee members; C = Central committee members).

Questions and Answers	M	S	L	C
Are you prepared to forego a raise if this would benefit low-income earners belonging to other unions?				
Yes	47%	56%	72%	88%
No	53	44	28	12
Total	100	100	100	100
	(N = 2,071)	(N = 241)	(N = 322)	(N = 250)
Higher paid groups within LO should support the low-income earners, even if this means that their own demands are set aside.				
Agree	78	85	87	94
Disagree	22	15	13	6
Total	100	100	100	100
	(N = 2,084)	(N = 241)	(N = 327)	(N = 249)
It is wrong for LO to make such wage demands that the least efficient industries are forced out of business.				
Agree	60	40	28	9
Disagree	40	60	72	91
Total	100	100	100	100
	(N = 2,029)	(N = 239)	(N = 327)	(N = 252)

whether the political elite represents exactly the views of the people. As far as the model of interactive democracy is concerned, such exact representativity is not desirable; instead, the elite should play an independent role in opinion-formation, and in certain cases, its duty should actually be one of opposition to public opinion. The justification for this view is founded in the supposition that public spirit is more widespread among the leadership than among the rank and file. It is the task of the leadership to influence the membership through propaganda in the direction of increased public spirit. The literature strongly supports the notion that public spirit is more widespread among the elite than among the people. Whether this is also the case within the Swedish trade union movement was something that had to be examined before such a claim could be made; it was first only a hypothesis. However, this hypothesis has now been tested, and it has, to a large extent, been confirmed because the measure of public spirit assumes ever greater values at the higher levels of the trade union hierarchy.

Activity

At the level of functional analysis, activity is the first democratic value of the variable "opinion-formation." Membership activity was measured by four operationalizations (phenomena 2–5, see tables 3.9–3.12).[11]

In the case of meeting attendance rate, 4 out of 10 members attended a union meeting during twelve months prior to the interview. Of those

Table 3.9. Meeting Attendance Rate: Membership Level (N = Total number).

Questions and Answers	Percentage
Have you attended a union meeting at any time during the last twelve months?	
Yes	39
No	61
Total	100
	(N = 2,161)
If yes:	
How many times?	
Once	9
Twice	12
Three times	3
Four times	4
Five–nine times	2
Ten times or more	1
"Every time"	1
No answer	7
Total	39
	(N = 2,161)
Did you speak up on any union-related issue at the meeting/meetings?	
Yes	15
No	22
No answer	2
Total	39
	(N = 2,161)

Table 3.10. Discussion of Union Matters: Membership Level (N = Total number).

Question and Answers	Percentage
Have you discussed union matters with a section committee member, district branch representative, or local committee member during the past four weeks?	
Yes	27
No	73
Total	100
	(N = 2,154)

who participated less than a half spoke on some union-related issue in the course of the meeting. More than a quarter discussed union matters with an official during the four weeks prior to the interview, and about the same number said that they regularly read most of the union periodical. The most exclusive activity—study—involved 1 member out of 10 during the year prior to the interview; the number rises dramatically to some 6 out of 10 at the local committee level.

For committee members four measures of activity (phenomena 4 and 6–8, see tables 3.11 and 3.13–3.15) were used. The foremost union activity of local committee members consisted of union-related work in general (committee meetings, writings, reading, and so forth). The study showed that the work week at the committee level allowed local committee members more opportunities for dealing with union issues during their working hours than was the case with committee members at the section level. Members at both levels had to spend additional time on union business outside their working hours; also in this case local committee members devoted more time to union-related work.

Table 3.11. Study Activity (N = Total number; M = Members; S = Section committee members; and L = Local committee members).

Question and Answers	M	S	L
Have you participated in a course or study circle devoted to union issues during the past twelve months?			
Yes	11%	58%	63%
No	89	42	37
Total	100	100	100
	(N = 2,139)	(N = 251)	(N = 330)

Table 3.12. Reading of Union Periodical: Membership Level (N = Total number).

Question and Answers	Percentage
How much of the union periodical do you read?	
Most of it	28
Part of it	49
Just leaf through it	17
Nothing	6
Total	100
	(N = 2,113)

Interactive democracy requires two-way communication between the membership and the leadership, and individual members must take an active interest in the union and exert influence within the local. In much the same way the committee members are expected to activate the rank and file by stimulating their interest through discussions and union-related informational activity. Tables 3.13, 3.14, and 3.15 indicate that most section and local committee members discussed union questions with at most 10 percent of the members during the course of a normal work week. Considering the much greater number represented by a

Table 3.13. Union-Related Work (N = Total number; S = Section committee members; and L = Local committee members).

Question and Answers	S	L
How many hours a week do you devote on the average to union-related work (meetings, writing, reading, and so forth)?		
During working hours		
0–2 hours	83%	65%
3–10 hours	12	20
At least 11 hours	5	15
Total	100	100
	(N = 218)	(N = 310)
Outside of working hours		
0–2 hours	58	33
3–10 hours	37	55
At least 11 hours	5	12
Total	100	100
	N = 213)	(N = 302)

Table 3.14. Discussion with Members (N = Total number; S = Section committee members; and L = Local committee members).

Question and Answers	S	L
With how many members of your section/local do you usually discuss union matters during a normal work week?		
0–0.9%	11%	35%
1.0–9.9%	60	52
10.0–24.9%	13	11
25.0–100.0%	16	3
Total	100	101[a]
	(N = 215)	(N = 283)

a. The sum is greater than 100 percent because of rounding to whole numbers.

committee member at the local level, the difference between the two levels is minimal; the tendency, when figured in percentages, favors the sectional leadership. In the case of informational activity, the results indicate that approximately 5 out of 10 section committee members, and 7 out of 10 of the local leadership provided information on union issues at work-place meetings or other union meetings.

Local leaders showed a somewhat higher percentage of participation than did sectional leaders in study activity, union-related work, and time devoted to dissemination of information. Considering the size of the unit represented, they also ranked higher in frequency of discussion of union matters. Thus, there was a slightly higher level of activity among the local leadership than among the section leadership.

Table 3.15. Informational Activity: Section and Local Committee Members (N = Total number; S = Section committee members; L = Local committee members).

Question and Answers	S	L
Have you provided information concerning union issues at a work place meeting or any other union meeting during the last month?		
Yes	51%	69%
No	49	31
Total	100	100
	(N = 249)	(N = 333)

Competence

The second democratic value of the variable "opinion-formation" is competence. In order to study membership knowledge of union matters (phenomenon 9) three questions requiring some knowledge of union issues were asked (table 3.16). A quarter of the membership was able to name the president of his or her union, approximately half was familiar with the contents of Paragraph 32 of the regulations of the Swedish Employers' Confederation, while only 4 percent knew that the provision on nonstrike agreements was set forth in the Collective Bargaining Law.

Leadership competence (phenomena 10–12, tables 3.17–3.19) was measured in several ways. The first operationalization of leadership competence is acquaintance with the membership. As might be expected, the officials of the smaller units, the sections, knew more members both by looks and by name than did the officers of the locals; the exact figures are indicated in table 3.17. A second requirement is that the leadership should be well suited to handle their union mandate. The text

Table 3.16. Membership Knowledge of Union Issues (N = Total number).

Questions and Answers	Percentage
What is the name of the president of your union?	
Right	26
Wrong, don't know, no answer	74
Total	100
	(N = 2,175)
What is contained in paragraph 32 of the regulations of the Swedish Employers' Confederation?	
Right	52
Wrong, don't know, no answer	48
Total	100
	(N = 2,177)
What is the name of the labor market law that contains the clause concerning the nonstrike agreement?	
Right	4
Wrong, don't know, no answer	96
Total	100
	(N = 2,177)

Table 3.17. Committee Members' Acquaintance with the Membership (N = Total number; S = Section committee members; L — Local committee members).

Question and Answers	S	L
How many of the members of your section/local do you know?		
Recognize—		
less than 20% of the membership	9%	33%
21–50%	11	25
51–70%	10	13
71–100%; "everybody"; "most"	69	29
Total	99a	100
	(N = 223)	(N = 315)
Know by name—		
less than 20% of the membership	15	45
21–50%	18	27
51–70%	4	9
71–100%; "everybody"; "most"	63	19
Total	100	100
	(N = 198)	(N = 291)

a. The sum is less than 100 percent because of rounding to whole numbers.

of the contract was selected as a test question. A comparison between the two levels gave the expected result: the ability to comprehend the agreement as written was higher at the higher level (table 3.18).

It is equally important that the union leadership be well informed concerning membership opinion. Table 3.19 measures leadership competence in this respect. The members were asked to express their opinions on six statements, while local and central leaders were asked to gauge membership response to these statements.[12] This process made it possible to determine whether the leadership was able to estimate cor-

Table 3.18. Understanding the Agreement (N = Total number; S = Section committee members; L = Local committee members).

Question and Answers	S	L
What is your opinion of the latest agreement?		
Generally easy to understand	30%	46%
Hard to understand in a few places	47	41
Hard to understand in quite a few places	17	10
Much too hard to understand as a whole	6	3
Total	100	100
	(N = 241)	(N = 326)

Table 3.19. The Leadership's Knowledge of Membership Opinion (N = Total number; L = Local committee members; C = Central committee members; percentage of correct estimates).

Issue	L	C
The leadership does not sufficiently consider the views of the individual worker.	14% (N = 326)	24% (N = 209)
Higher paid groups within LO should support the low-income earners even if this means that their own demands are set aside.	28 (N = 324)	39 (N = 230)
It is wrong for LO to make such demands that the least efficient industries are forced out of business.	37 (N = 314)	18 (N = 212)
The union managed to derive maximum benefits from the latest negotiated agreement.	48 (N = 324)	43 (N = 235)
Sweden is still a class society.	48 (N = 321)	37 (N = 220)
Collective affiliation is wrong.	56 (N = 312)	42 (N = 231)

rectly membership opinion. For the first statement, only 14 percent of the local officials were able to judge correctly the membership response to the statement that the leadership does not sufficiently consider the views of the individual worker; the central level fares somewhat better with 24 percent. Officials improved their performances in the five subsequent assertions. On two of the statements the central leadership proved the better judge of membership opinion; on four, the local officials.

However, the resulting figures are highly dependent on what the tolerable margin of error is. With a margin of ± 15 percent, the result thus depends on rather subjective decisions, and too close attention should not be paid to the actual numbers. These figures assume a new and different importance in the comparative analysis of the 50 locals. There, leadership competence varies from one local to another, according to political, social, and economic variables.

Other, more objectively reliable results illustrating the process of opinion-formation at the elite level in democratic organizations may be determined by further exploration of the data that relate to leadership competence.[13] Wherever possible, the opinions of the officials will be compared with the opinions of the membership and the leadership's estimation of membership opinion.

The first statement (table 3.27, second question) shows that only a small percentage of the local and central leadership believed that the members thought that not enough attention was paid to the views of the individual worker. In fact, more than half of the membership held that opinion. Both levels thus proved to be poor judges of membership opinion, possibly swayed by wishful thinking. The second statement (table 3.8, second question) finds both levels anxious to support low-income groups; the same is true of the membership, although not quite to the same extent. In this case, the central leadership displayed a more realistic view of membership opinion than did the local leaders, who underestimated the public spirit of the rank and file. On statement three, "wage demands—resulting industrial failures" (table 3.8, third question), widely divergent views among the three levels were found; the rank and file was the most critical of the consequences of the wage policy, the local leadership less so, and the central leadership hardly at all. Union officials are often deluded into thinking that the rank and file holds the same opinions as they do. Central leaders also proved to be poor judges of membership opinion, the leaders of the locals somewhat better. As for the fourth statement, whether the union managed to derive maximum benefit from the most recent bargaining session (table 3.39, first question), the central leadership appeared reasonably satisfied, while the two lower levels were dissatisfied. Because the tendency to ascribe their own views to the membership prevailed also in this case, local officials achieved somewhat better figures than did the central leadership. On statement number five concerning a class society (table 3.39, second question), the local leaders were more radical in their views than either the rank and file or the central leadership and correctly estimated membership opinion. The central leadership underestimated the radicalism of the members. Finally, on collective affiliation (table 3.37, fifth question), both levels erroneously believed that the rank and file shared their general views. The central leadership, accepting affiliation, scored lower than the local leadership, being critical of affiliation.

Thus, these figures reveal a tendency for trade union officials to believe that the rank and file shares their opinions. The way in which the leaders perceive membership opinion is often predicated upon wishful thinking and a tendency to idealize membership attitudes toward the trade union movement.

System Orientation

The third value of the variable "opinion-formation" is labeled system orientation. This value has been made operational through numerous questions put to the membership (phenomena 13–19, see tables 3.20–3.27), and to officials (phenomenon 15, see table 3.22; phenomenon 17, see table 3.25; and phenomena 20–21, see tables 3.28–3.29).

Related to this value is the question why the member joined the union movement in the first place. More specifically, it was necessary to determine the empirical foundation for the criticism leveled against the trade union movement that members join out of conformism, or a sense of compulsion, and to compare this reason for joining with other, from the union's point of view, more positive motivations, such as feelings of solidarity. It appears from table 3.20 that a quarter of those interviewed cited conformism or a sense of compulsion as a reason for joining. It should be noted in this connection that the reason least flattering to the trade union movement, the sense of compulsion, was mentioned by as many as 18 percent of the respondents. The most frequently stated reason for joining was that membership in a union was thought to be useful.[14] The one often cited by apologists of the workers' movement, a sense of solidarity, was mentioned by somewhat more than a quarter of the membership. The figure for this, the best answer from a normative and democratic point of view, was thus roughly the same as the figures for discussion of union matters, reading of union periodicals, and ability to name the union president.

How are workers who remain outside the trade unions treated? Table 3.21 shows that as many as 21 percent of those interviewed had noticed some form of harassment directed against the outsiders. In most cases, this took the form of "snide remarks and verbal pressure." Sometimes it became more serious. Under the heading "punitive actions by members" there were "anonymous letters," "threats of beatings," and "verbal abuse and violent actions"; under the title "punitive actions by union leadership," "threats by the committee and by the representative," "attempts to transfer the worker to another place of work," and "frozen out by the shop steward at the place of work."

Table 3.20. Reason for Joining the Union: Members (N = Total number).

Question and Answers	Percentage
People belong to trade unions for different reasons. What prompted you to join?	
Most of the others belong	7%
I felt compelled to join	18
I find it useful to belong	45
Solidarity with the workers' movement	27
Practicality and solidarity combined	2
Other reasons	1
Total	100
	(N = 2,138)

Table 3.21. Harassment: Members (N = Total number).

Questions and Answers	Percentage
Have you ever noticed that a person who does not belong to the union has been subjected to harassment or abuse?	
Yes	21
No	79
Total	100
	(N = 2,139)
If yes, what kind?	
Snide remarks and verbal pressure	14
Freezing out	1
Punitive actions by members	3
Punitive actions by leaders	1
No answer	2
Total	21
	(N = 2,139)

The most hotly debated issue concerning the union movement and system orientation is that of the collective affiliation of local unions with the Social Democratic Party. Table 3.22 indicates that a clear majority of the membership (64 percent) considered collective affiliation with the Social Democrats an undesirable form of political party affiliation. Also within the section and local leadership a majority opposed collective affiliation. Only the central level favored this affiliation.

Leading Social Democratic circles defend the practice of collective affiliation by pointing to the right of disclaimer. Table 3.23 indicates that

Table 3.22. Attitude toward Collective Affiliation (N = Total number; M = Members; S = Section committee members; L = Local committee members; C = Central committee members).

Question and Answers	M	S	L	C
Collective affiliation with the Social Democratic Party is an undesirable form of political party affiliation.				
Agree	64%	52%	56%	33%
Disagree	36	48	44	67
Total	100	100	100	100
	(N = 1,957)	(N = 241)	(N = 327)	(N = 252)

Table 3.23. Political Party Preferences and Disclaimers among Collectively Affiliated Members (N = Total number).

Political Party	Those Who Have Not Disclaimed Affiliation	Those Who Have Disclaimed Affiliation
Conservative	2%	0%
Liberal	3	1
Center party	6	0
"Non-socialist parties"	2	0
Social Democratic	61	1
Communists	5	2
Don't know, no preference, no answer	16	1
Total	95%	5%
	(N = 1,371)	

only 5 percent of the members in the collectively affiliated locals took advantage of this right, primarily members with Communist Party sympathies but also Liberals and Social Democrats. Of non–Social Democratic union members those belonging to the Center Party appeared to be relatively more willing to accept collective affiliation with the Social Democratic Party. Remarkably few disclaimed party affiliation. Eighteen percent of the total number interviewed were collectively affiliated without protest despite non-socialist or Communist Party sympathies (table 3.23); if we include those undecided or of unknown party preference we arrive at a total of more than a third. Because 18 percent of the collectively affiliated members did not use the right of disclaimer even though they favored a party other than the Social Democrats, the collective affiliation of trade union locals with the Social Democratic Party constitutes a violation of the democratic principle of minority rights.

System orientation within the union movement thus presents rather a bleak picture: 18 percent of the rank and file belonged to the labor union because they felt compelled to; 21 percent had noticed some form of harassment; a majority of the membership and the local leadership dissociated themselves from the common and officially defended practice of collective affiliation with the Social Democratic Party; the right to disclaim affiliation did not work in actuality; and 18 percent of collectively affiliated union members who had not disclaimed affiliation actually sympathized with other political parties.

Other measures of system orientation also present a rather negative picture of the individual member's view of the trade union system. A full

Table 3.24. Membership Attitudes toward the System of Representation (N = Total number).

Question and Answers	Percentage
The system of representation including central negotiations, representatives, and steering committees at various levels should be abolished.	
Agree	32
Disagree	68
Total	100
	(N = 1,991)

third of the membership held the extreme opinion that "the system of representation including central negotiations, representatives, and steering committees at various levels should be abolished" (table 3.24). Somewhat more than half of the membership found the top officials guilty of bossism (table 3.25); within section and local committees the figure was lower, but still comparatively high. More than half found the representatives too influential when compared to ordinary members and elected officials (table 3.26). The rank and file showed more confidence in sectional and local committee members, even though the local leadership was criticized for not paying sufficient attention to the views of the individual worker (table 3.27).

Table 3.28 measures the "idealism" of the union officials, in order to test the empirical basis for the accusation that the trade union movement nowadays is primarily regarded as a stepping-stone for the industrial worker intent on making a career within the unions rather than an undertaking based on idealism or a sense of duty. The table indicates that

Table 3.25. Attitudes toward Top Officials (N = Total number; M = Members; S = Section committee members; L = Local committee members).

Question and Answers	M	S	L
It is justified to accuse the steering committee of the national union and the top officials within LO of bossism.			
Agree	59%	45%	35%
Disagree	41	55	65
Total	100	100	100
	(N = 2,028)	(N = 244)	(N = 322)

Table 3.26. Membership Attitudes toward Representatives (N = Total number).

Question and Answers	Percentage
The representatives are too influential when compared to ordinary members and elected committee members.	
Agree	55
Disagree	45
Total	100
	(N = 2,013)

everybody at the two local committee levels and 3 out of 4 persons at the central level believed that their fellow committee members really were inspired by a sense of duty and idealism. This would seem to refute the criticism mentioned earlier. Far more interesting are the differences that are found between the local and central levels of leadership. These differences are especially noticeable when we consider the alternative answer "more pleasant and stimulating tasks; careerism": an overwhelming majority at the central level selected this alternative; only a few at the local levels. Thus, although the central level tends to show a generally higher frequency of "democratic responses," whenever such a possibility can be said to exist, in this case, the lower levels more often cited "ideal-

Table 3.27. Membership Confidence in Local Leadership (N = Total number).

Questions and Answers	Percentage
Section and local committees handle issues in a way that inspires confidence.	
Agree	70
Disagree	30
Total	100
	(N = 2,032)
Section and local committees do not sufficiently consider the views of the individual worker.	
Agree	58
Disagree	42
Total	100
	(N = 2,066)

Table 3.28. Idealism of Committee Members (N = Total number; S = Section committee members; L = Local committee members; C = Central committee members).

Question and Answers	S	L	C
What do you think motivates the candidates for positions on the section, local, or national committee to run for office?[a]			
They view the position as providing a more pleasant and stimulating task; careerism.	22%	28%	83%
The foremost motivating force is idealism, a sense of duty; pressure from fellow workers.	100	100	76
Total	(N = 231)	(N = 330)	(N = 249)

a. The sum may be greater than 100 percent because both alternatives may be chosen.

ism" or "duty" as the foremost motivating force behind a position within the union. How should this be interpreted? The probable explanation is that a position of trust at a lower level means primarily sacrifice, whereas work at the central level offers stimulation and a definite change for the better for the individual official. At the central level the individual union career has been crowned with success—the initial effort has led to the top—whereas many of the local leaders probably lack the drive necessary to devote all their efforts toward a union career.

Interactive democracy requires a constant exchange between leadership and members during the opinion-forming process. How do the decision-making committee members view membership activity (table 3.29)? The low level of union activity was considered by all three levels as one of the most serious problems facing the trade union movement today. The problem was viewed as less serious by the central level than by the local leadership levels. However, an increase in membership activity might bring new problems: for example, the governing committee might find its ability to act curtailed. Committee members were asked what they thought of this, and the answer showed that the lower the leadership level and the closer to the membership an official was, the more he believed that most of his colleagues on the committee would be unwilling to work toward an increase in membership activity if this in turn would curtail the ability of the elected representatives to act. The higher levels, removed from daily contact with the general membership, could afford to view increased membership activity more positively.

Legitimacy

The ideal consequence of interaction during the opinion-formation process would be consensus between members and leadership. The first

Table 3.29. Attitude of Committee Members toward Membership Activity (N = Total number; S = Section committee members; L = Local committee members; C = Central committee members).

Questions and Answers	S	L	C
The low level of union activity among the membership is one of the most serious problems facing the trade union movement of today.			
Agree	94%	93%	72%
Disagree	6	7	28
Total	100	100	100
	(N = 240)	(N = 329)	(N = 250)
Most committee members at the section, local, or national level would be unwilling to work to increase membership activity if this in turn would curtail the ability of elected officials and representatives to act.			
Agree	46	21	11
Disagree	54	79	89
Total	100	100	100
	(N = 237)	(N = 320)	(N = 249)

democratic value included in the variable "consensus-building" is labeled legitimacy (phenomenon 22, see tables 3.30–3.33 and tables 3.34–3.36). Are the officers chosen in a manner acceptable to the general membership (table 3.30)? Seventy-four percent of the membership criticized union elections, frequently because of the limited choice of candidates and platforms, and the tendency for the same officers to be reelected again and again, and thus stay in office too long. Some members found certain groups underrepresented (primarily women and political dissidents). Only a little more than a quarter of the members were satisfied with the election procedure. Once more the most normatively democratically "correct" answer was represented by 25 percent.

Does this statistic constitute an adequate measure of legitimacy? For awareness, criticism, and dissatisfaction are also democratic assets. Should democratic desiderata in the case of legitimacy be represented only by those who are satisfied and uncritical? How is it possible to know whether it is, in fact, political apathy, rather than legitimacy, that is being measured?

This objection was tested by comparing the activity level of the noncritical respondents with the activity level of the total number of respondents in seven additional respects. The result showed very little difference between the noncritical category and the average. When it

Table 3.30. Legitimacy: Members (N = Total number).

Questions and Answers		Percentage
Are you critical of any aspect of union elections?		
Yes		74
No		26
Total		100
		(N = 1,947)
If yes:[a]		
The officers are reelected too often and stay in office too long		29
Too few candidates		37
Too few differences in platforms		31
Certain groups are underrepresented		10
Women	2	
Political dissidents	2	
Special job categories	1	
Low-income groups	1	
Immigrants	1	
The young	1	
Those who find it hard to speak up	1	
Others	1	
Subtotal	10	
The elections should be held in a different place.		3
At the place of work	2	
Others	1	
Subtotal	3	
Other criticism		2
Nomination procedure	1	
Other	1	
Subtotal	2	
		(N = 1,947)

a. The sum is greater than 74 percent because more than one answer may be given.

comes to meeting attendance rate, discussion of union matters, and the most exclusive activity measure, study activity, the noncritical group was somewhat more active than the average; in reading the union publication, attitude toward a wage policy of solidarity, and dissatisfaction with the union they were correspondingly somewhat less active than the average. Thus, the measure of legitimacy was found to be valid.[15]

The choice of legitimacy as a democratic value was inspired by Schumpeter's notion of political competition. Competition was to prevent the rise of an oligarchy and further an election procedure that the membership perceived as legitimate. Does it really work this way? Does competition further legitimacy? It was necessary to test the question empirically because there might conceivably be instances in which the membership accepts the election procedure even though there is a dearth of candidates competing. On the other hand, there might also be membership unhappiness with a competitive situation. However, the interviews brought out that the most frequently voiced reason for dissatisfaction with union elections was lack of competition.

Table 3.31 again reflects a numerical increase in the number of contested elections at the upper echelons of the union hierarchy. Thirty-four percent at the section level, 49 percent at the local, and 75 percent at the central level had to compete for their seats. The same table shows that, at all three levels, the main difference between the individual candidates was confined to "personality." Differences of political opinion appeared to play a relatively insignificant role. At the central level, occupation was of great importance.

At union congresses there are special election committees, the task of which is the careful planning of the elections. But at the local level the

Table 3.31. Contested Union Elections (N = Total number; S = Section committee members; L = Local committee members; C = Central committee members).

Question and Answers	S	L	C
Did you have to compete for your seat when you were elected to the committee?			
Yes	34%	49%	75%
No	66	51	25
Total	100	100	100
	(N = 235)	(N = 325)	(N = 243)
If yes:			
What was the difference between the various candidates?			
Their political views	5	7	3
Their occupation	2	2	26
Experience in union work	1	4	2
Personality only	21	29	34
Other things	3	1	4
No answer	2	5	5
Total	34	48[a]	74[a]
	(N = 235)	(N = 325)	(N = 243)

a. The sum is less than 49 percent and 75 percent because of rounding to whole numbers.

Table 3.32. Nomination and Reelection within the Locals (N = Total number; S = Section committee members; L = Local committee members).

Questions and Answers	S	L
Why did you run for office the first time?		
I was asked by the representative/someone already on the committee.	37%	36%
My name was proposed by fellow workers not themselves on the committee.	63	63
Total	100	99[a]
	(N = 235)	(N = 325)
When were you first elected to the committee?		
1970 on	52	42
1965–1969	23	25
1960–1964	16	11
1956–1959	4	4
Prior to 1955	6	19
Total	101[a]	101[a]
	(N = 139)	(N = 249)

a. The sum is less or greater than 100 percent because of rounding to whole numbers.

initiative in most cases is not, as might be expected, taken by the committee or by the representatives. According to table 3.32, most candidates to sectional and local offices were nominated by fellow workers who were not themselves on the committee. The same table also shows the average length of tenure of the committee members. Roughly half of the committee members (somewhat less on the local level) had held office for four years or less.

The actual test of the hypothesis concerning the correlation between legitimacy and competition is carried out in table 3.33. There the union members studied were divided into two groups. The first group included the members of locals with contested elections; the second group com-

Table 3.33. Legitimacy and Competition in Union Elections (N = Total number).

Category	Noncritical Members
Locals with competition	25%
	(N = 1,072)
Locals with no competition	28
	(N = 875)
All locals	26
	(N = 1,947)

prised members from locals with uncontested elections. Legitimacy was examined in the same manner as for the group as a whole. If the former group also scored better on measures of legitimacy, it would tend to confirm Schumpeter's model of competition.

The table indicates that this was not the case. In the locals with contested elections 25 percent of the membership expressed satisfaction with the election procedure; in those with uncontested elections the figure was 28 percent (26 percent for all locals). These figures are very close; any discernible tendency runs counter to the trend expected according to Schumpeter's theories. Thus, competition does not further legitimacy as Schumpeter envisioned in his model of democracy.

Schumpeter's elegant competition model has—as was mentioned in chapter one—greatly influenced political science research during the last few decades. One might add that it has apparently influenced the political views of many trade union members because a quarter of those interviewed checked off the answer that there should be more candidates to select from in union elections (table 3.30). In *Folket och eliterna* the competition model was criticized primarily from a normative point of view because it appeared to place greater emphasis on the political elites and less on the participation of the masses than the classic democratic doctrine had assumed. It is now possible to criticize that model also from a functional point of view: competition within the Swedish trade union movement does not appear to further democratic legitimacy.

Finally, who is elected to the trade union leadership? Table 3.34

Table 3.34. Union Leaders: Political Data (N = Total number; M = Members; S = Section committee members; L = Local committee members; C = Central committee members).

Question and Answers	M	S	L	C
What is your political party preference?				
Conservative	2%	0%	0%	0%
Liberal	4	0	1	0
Center Party	10	3	4	0
"Non-socialist parties"	2	0	0	0
Social Democrats	70	93	90	98
Communists	8	4	5	1
Christian Democratic Union	1	0	0	0
Don't know; none	3	1	0	1
Total	100	101[a]	100	100
	(N = 1,876)	(N = 240)	(N = 310)	(N = 250)

a. The sum is greater than 100 percent because of rounding to whole numbers.

Table 3.35. "Red, Pink, and White Social Democrats" (N = Total number; M = Members; S = Section committee members; L = Local committee members; C = Central committee members).[a]

Choice	M	S	L	C
Red	14%	17%	18%	13%
Pink	67	62	74	83
White	19	21	9	3
Total	100	100	101[b]	99[b]
	(N = 1,308)	(N = 223)	(N = 279)	(N = 246)

a. "Red" = Communist party as second party choice; "pink" = could not make a second party choice; "white" = non-socialist party as second party choice.

b. The sum is greater or smaller than 100 percent because of rounding to whole numbers.

indicates the overwhelming position of the Social Democrats among the elected officials: 90 percent or more, compared to 70 percent among the rank and file. In order to differentiate among the large block of Social Democrats, they have been divided in table 3.35 into "red" members (those who selected the Communist Party as their second choice), "pink" members (those who could not make a second party choice), and "white" members (those who selected a non-socialist party as their second choice). By breaking down the sample in this way, it is possible again to distinguish a trace of the familiar pattern: except for a dip among the sectional leadership, the proportion of "pink" Social Democrats rises in the higher levels of the hierarchy. In the case of the "red" Social Democrats, the middle levels proved to be more radical, with the central level closer to the rank and file. The "white" proportion decreases significantly at the higher levels.

Table 3.36 concerns the social background of union officials. The father's occupation seems to be unimportant: "worker" is remarkably evenly represented at all levels. On the other hand, again the numbers ascend from the membership level, via the local, to the central level when questions about the father's affiliation with a union and which party he voted for were asked. Trade union leaders, especially at the higher level, generally had a union member and a Social Democrat for a father.

Agreement of Opinion

The second democratic value of the variable "consensus-building" is labeled agreement of opinion (phenomenon 23, see tables 3.37–3.38). This is the most important value for consensus-building and one of the more

Table 3.36. Union Leaders: Social Data (N = Total number; M = Members; S = Section committee members; L = Local committee members; C = Central committee members).

Questions and Answers	M	S	L	C
What is/was your father's occupation?				
Farmer	20%	24%	16%	15%
Self-employed; civil servant	15	15	16	17
Agricultural worker	3	5	9	5
Worker (other than agricultural)	52	50	50	52
Lower clerk; worker outside LO area	9	5	9	10
Don't know; retired; father unknown	1	1	1	2
Total	100	100	101[a]	101[a]
	(N = 1,990)	(N = 232)	(N = 319)	(N = 249)
Does/did your father belong to a trade union?				
Yes	54	62	70	76
No	30	27	26	18
Don't know	15	11	4	7
Total	99[a]	100	100	101[a]
	(N = 2,035)	(N = 242)	(N = 320)	(N = 248)
Which party does/did your father vote for?				
Conservative	3	3	1	2
Liberal	8	5	6	3
Center Party	9	6	6	3
"Non-socialist parties"	4	0	2	0
Social Democrats	48	66	62	80
Communists	1	5	7	3
Don't know; none	27	16	16	9
Total	100	101[a]	100	100
	(N = 1,820)	(N = 217)	(N = 303)	(N = 243)

a. The sum is less or greater than 100 percent because of rounding to whole numbers.

important values in the interactive democracy model as a whole. Radical critics of the union movement maintain that bossism exists in the sense that the leaders do not represent the consensus of the membership. This claim was examined with five questions.

No alternative answers were given to the first question in table 3.37. The respondent was asked to indicate which issues he thought should receive priority treatment by the section or local. The answers are listed in

Table 3.37. Agreement of Opinion: Response Frequencies (N — Total number; M = Members; S = Section committee members; L = Local committee members; C = Central committee members).

Questions and Answers	M	S	L	C
Which issues should, in your opinion, receive priority treatment by the section or local?[a]				
Higher wages	48%	39%	45%	—
Equalization of wages	7	6	7	—
Monthly pay	2	1	2	—
Work environment	53	51	52	—
Job security	10	12	13	—
Working hours	4	4	5	—
Occupational training	2	0	5	—
Union activity	15	36	42	—
Industrial democracy	3	6	16	—
Political matters	2	8	6	—
Ridding unions of politics	1	0	0	—
	(N = 1,504)	(N = 220)	(N = 305)	—
What should, in your view, be the main objective of the union movement?[a]				
Increased worker representation on the governing board	61	73	77	72
Price and wage freeze	72	56	38	18
Equal pay for equal work regardless of financial state of industry	93	78	80	78
Nationalization of banks and large industry	26	50	45	50
The people should take over the means of production	19	24	31	39
Increase the profitability of industry	15	13	12	11
	(N = 1,621)	(N = 247)	(N = 326)	(N = 240)
Higher paid groups within LO should support the low-income earners even if this means that their own demands are set aside.				
Agree	78	85	87	94
Disagree	22	15	13	6
Total	100	100	100	100
	(N = 2,084)	(N = 241)	(N = 327)	(N = 249)

Table 3.37 (*continued*)

Questions and Answers	M	S	L	C
It is wrong for LO to make such wage demands that the least efficient industries are forced out of business.				
Agree	60	40	28	9
Disagree	40	60	72	91
Total	100	100	100	100
	(N = 2,029)	(N = 239)	(N = 327)	(N = 252)
Collective affiliation with the Social Democratic Party is an undesirable form of political party affiliation.				
Agree	64	52	56	33
Disagree	36	48	44	67
Total	100	100	100	100
	(N = 1,957)	(N = 241)	(N = 327)	(N = 252)

a. The sum is greater than 100 percent because more than one answer may be given.

three columns: by membership, section, and local officials; this question was not asked at the central level. The two issues most often mentioned were wages and working environment. Equalization of wages was not included under the heading wage increase, but was coded separately. Interest in this issue was rather limited. A comparison of the three columns line by line gives the general impression of extensive agreement between membership opinion and the views of the leadership, with the exceptions of union activity and industrial democracy.

The second question offered six choices concerning the main objective of the labor union movement, according to the respondent. "Equal pay for equal work regardless of the financial state of the industry" was the most frequently cited answer at all levels. At the membership level "price and wage freeze," and "increased worker representation on the governing board" were two popular alternatives. Although a price and wage freeze is in direct conflict with the official platform of the trade union movement, almost three-fourths of the membership selected this alternative. The percentage decreases in the higher levels of union hierarchy. However, increased worker representation proved to be a popular choice also among the leadership. In the case of the two radical alternatives, "nationalization of banks and large industry" and "the people should take over the means of production," a fourth and fifth respectively of the members rose to 50 and somewhat less than 40 percent at

the higher levels of the hierarchy. Thus, approximately half of the union
leadership supports the demand for nationalization.

The three remaining questions reflect agreement or disagreement with
two statements about a wage policy of solidarity and one about collective affiliation. There was strong support for the low-income earners at
all levels; on the question of responsibility for the economic consequences of the wage policy, however, membership and leadership di-
verged, especially members and central leaders; on the question of
collective affiliation there were also certain differences of opinion.

What do the answers provided by members and leadership to these
five questions reveal about agreement of opinion within the Swedish
labor union movement? In order to arrive at a conclusion statistical
methods were used to compare the opinion structure of the various levels
and to establish an index for each question as a measure of agreement
(table 3.38). Representativity of opinion for sectional committee members was arrived at by extracting those members who belong to locals
with sections or clubs ("Ms" in table 3.38: N = 795, 1,110, 1,080, and
1,040, respectively, in the five questions). In the first two questions, both
with several possible answers, Robinson's Index of Agreement was used;
this scale ranges from 0.000 (no agreement) to 1.000 (perfect agreement).[16] The result indicates a high level of agreement of opinion, with
index values between 0.763 and 0.961. For technical reasons, it is not
possible to apply Robinson's Index to the last three questions, which have
only two possible answers. Thus, an index was formulated in the following way: 100 minus the difference in percentage between the two levels
being compared (using one decimal); the obtained difference was divided
by 100. Once again, the index values are high. The leadership is highly
representative of membership opinion in its advocacy of support for the
low-income earners. There is somewhat less agreement with the mem-

Table 3.38. Agreement of Opinion: Index (M = Members; Ms = Members
in locals containing sections; S = Section committee members; L = Local
committee members).

Questions[a]	Ms/S	M/L	M/C
Priority issues	0.961	0.936	—
Union objective	0.878	0.880	0.763
Support for low-income earners	0.922	0.912	0.833
Wage demands—resulting industrial failures	0.796	0.674	0.491
Collective affiliation	0.886	0.921	0.694

a. For the precise wording of the questions, see table 3.37.

bership on the economic consequences of the high wage demands, especially at the central level. The representativity values for collective affiliation fall somewhere in between, but are still high. Table 3.38 also indicates that the agreement index generally declines at the higher levels of the union hierarchy. Summing up, there exists a high degree of agreement between the members and leadership of the Swedish trade union movement.

Demands

Within an interactive democracy membership dissatisfaction and demands that the leadership advance the positions of the movement are positive values. Membership dissatisfaction was measured in different ways (phenomena 24–25, see tables 3.39–3.40). Table 3.39 shows that 61 percent of the membership was dissatisfied with the outcome of the agreement prior to the fieldwork. Dissatisfaction was higher at the local committee level. Only at the central level did the majority think that the unions managed to extract the maximum number of concessions from the employers.

In order to determine whether dissatisfaction with the union corresponded to a general radical view of society, members were asked if they

Table 3.39. Membership Demands and Leadership Opinion: A Comparison (N = Total number; M = Members; S = Section committee members; L = Local committee members; C = Central committee members).

Questions and Answers	M	S	L	C.
The union managed to derive maximum benefits from the latest negotiated agreement.				
Agree	39%	19%	33%	67%
Disagree	61	81	67	33
Total	100	100	100	100
	(N = 2,041)	(N = 248)	(N = 325)	(N = 248)
Sweden is still a class society.				
Agree	84	88	89	83
Disagree	16	12	11	17
Total	100	100	100	100
	(N = 2,100)	(N = 247)	(N = 330)	(N = 248)
Correlation between union dissatisfaction and a radical view of society (the two questions above)	$\Phi = 0.183$	$\Phi = 0.132$	$\Phi = 0.177$	$\Phi = 0.024$

considered Sweden still to be a class society.[17] A considerable majority at all levels agreed; sectional and local officials proved somewhat more radical than both the rank and file and the central leadership.

The correlation between union dissatisfaction and a radical view at all four levels was tested by calculating phi coefficients; at the three lower levels the correlation was confirmed at a 1 percent level by means of a chi^2 test; at the central level there is no correlation. This may be interpreted in the following way: at the three lower levels a radical view of society leads to dissatisfaction with the union to a large extent. The central level is as radical as the rank and file,[18] but this radicalism does not lead to dissatisfaction with the union in the same way; the central leadership's view of the agreement is seemingly influenced by something other than value judgments of society. The most plausible explanation is that the bargaining function of the central leadership has given the central committee members a different view of reality from the one held by the general membership. Because officials at the central level directly confront the opponent during the negotiations, they, regardless of what concessions they would like to extract, are also able to determine what realistically might be expected from the employers.

In addition, a more general question was asked: are there issues which, in the opinion of the membership, are neglected by the section or the local? Then, the section and local committee members were asked to gauge membership opinion on this point (table 3.40). Once more, the familiar series of ascending numbers indicates that committee members at the section, local, and central levels were increasingly inclined to think that membership dissatisfaction on this issue was more widespread than it actually was. Whereas 35 percent of the rank and file were of the opinion that there were questions that were neglected by the section or local, almost twice that number among the officials at the central level thought that the general membership was dissatisfied.

Table 3.40 indicates what specific questions the members considered neglected and which of them the leadership thought that the membership would pick. On the whole, the leadership had a rather accurate view of membership demands. On certain issues the officials tended to overestimate membership dissatisfaction. Thus wages were mentioned almost three times as often at the central level as among the rank and file; the leaders at the central level were well aware of the difference of opinion that existed between them and the members on the question of wage agreements. A preference for monthly salaries, a shorter work week, industrial democracy, and certain reforms predicated on political decisions were also mentioned more frequently by the leadership than by the members.

Table 3.40. "Neglected Issues": Leadership and Membership Opinions (N = Total number; M = Members; S = Section committee members; L = Local committee members; C = Central committee members).

Questions and Answers	M	S	L	C
In your opinion, are there any questions which the members consider important and which the section/local/union has neglected? (asked of levels S, L, and C)				
Are there any questions which you think are neglected by the section/local? (asked of level M)				
Yes	35%	41%	51%	67%
No	65	59	49	33
Total	100	100	100	100
	(N = 1,899)	(N = 239)	(N = 313)	(N = 244)
If yes, which questions?[a]				
Higher wages	6	12	11	16
Equalization of wages	6	1	5	8
Monthly pay	1	4	1	9
Work environment	10	8	16	13
Job security	3	2	3	3
Working hours	1	3	6	10
Occupational training	1	0	2	1
Union activity	11	10	13	15
Industrial democracy	1	0	7	5
Political matters	0	0	2	6
Ridding unions of politics	1	0	0	0
	(N = 1,899)	(N = 239)	(N = 313)	(N = 244)
In your view what is it that prevents the section/local/union from resolving these issues?[a]				
The employer	–	15	15	23
LO; the union	–	5	8	8
The local/section representative	–	4	5	2
The members	–	7	7	16
Size of organization (too small)	–	6	12	10
Size of organization (too large)	–	1	0	0
Not within union's jurisdiction	–	7	12	21
New issue, still under investigation	–	0	2	3
	–	(N = 239)	(N = 313)	(N = 244)

a. Several answers may be selected. The second and third questions thus add up to more than the total number of affirmative answers in the first question.

Table 3.40 also indicates opinions on the reason why these questions
had been neglected (a question asked only at the leadership level). The
central level, which was most inclined to perceive the rank and file as
dissatisfied, was also most apt to blame forces outside the unions for this
discontent: the employer was mentioned more often, as were the too limited formal powers of the union. This level was also more inclined than
the other levels to blame the membership for the inability of the union
movement to deal with certain questions. The section and local officers
also mentioned, although less often, the employer, the authority of the
unions, and the general membership as the reasons why certain questions
were neglected. They also displayed a remarkable degree of self-criti-
cism in placing the blame on their own local sections or representatives.

Schooling

In building consensus in an interactive democracy, it is the primary task
of the membership to offer criticism and make demands, whereas the
main role of the leadership is to educate the members by means of information and propaganda to the objectives of the movement. Just how successful the leadership has been in this schooling process (phenomenon
26) is shown in table 3.41. Throughout the table the percentage of answers in line with the ideology of LO rises in upper echelons of the union
hierarchy.

Table 3.41. Attitude toward Union Ideology: Percentages of Agreement with the Official
Opinion of LO (N = Total number; M = Members; S = Section committee members;
L = Local committee members; C = Central committee members).

Official Opinion of LO	M	S	L	C
It is not too easy to receive social welfare benefits.	27% (N = 2,081)	38% (N = 245)	48% (N = 321)	75% (N = 246)
The State should pursue the present-day immigration policy and not give Swedish workers job priority.	12 (N = 2,106)	16 (N = 248)	24 (N = 322)	42 (N = 242)
Higher paid groups within LO should support the low-income earners even if this means that their own demands are set aside.	78 (N = 2,084)	85 (N = 241)	87 (N = 327)	94 (N = 249)
It is not wrong for LO to make such wage demands that the least efficient industries are forced out of business.	40 (N = 2,029)	60 (N = 239)	72 (N = 327)	91 (N = 252)

First, only a little more than a quarter of the members shared the official opinion of LO that it is not too easy to receive social welfare benefits. Second, no more than 12 percent of the workers endorsed the liberal immigration policy of the workers' movement; not even a majority of the central level agreed with that policy. The questions concerning a wage policy of solidarity fared better. Thus, third, there was very strong support for the official championing of low-income earners and, fourth, there was somewhat less enthusiasm among the membership for the economic consequences of high wage demands.

Because an interactive democracy assigns an independent role of opinion-formation to the leadership vis-à-vis the members, officials sometimes find themselves forced to oppose membership opinion during this ideological schooling process and give proof of a conception of leadership (phenomenon 27). Table 3.42 shows that most union leaders did possess this conception. Willingness to assume leadership responsibility in the face of any reactionary trends among the workers increased at higher levels of the hierarchy. The figures are actually so high that it would be tempting to undertake a comparative study in order to ascertain whether any other Swedish organization can show higher figures for the value conception of leadership.

Decision and Nondecision

Are the decisions taken by the leadership in line with the ideal consensus that has been reached between leaders and members? As mentioned in chapter 1, the American theorists P. Bachrach and M. Baratz maintain

Table 3.42. Conception of Leadership (N = Total number; S = Section committee members; L = Local committee members; C = Central committee members).

Question and Answers	S	L	C
It is not always necessary for the leaders to represent exactly the views of the membership. In some cases it may be more important that the leaders oppose any reactionary tendencies among the members.			
Agree	75%	82%	85%
Disagree	25	18	15
Total	100	100	100
	(N = 240)	(N = 326)	(N = 251)

that it is important to study not differences of opinion or conflicts among different groups, but rather any issues neglected by the leadership in the decision-making process, despite membership interest. The demand by a small party on the Swedish extreme left that the union be made a fighting organization is interpreted to mean that it should be the responsibility of the leadership to make certain that membership demands are acted on without consideration for anything outside local membership opinion, be it union coordination, agreements with the employer, or state regulations (phenomenon 28).

To what extent do the questionnaires show membership opinion in the 50 locals as resulting in decisions by the committee, and to what extent as resulting in nondecisions? Membership views on section or local priorities were coded in eleven categories (see tables 3.37 and 3.40). These opinions were counted by local, and thus a matrix containing 11 × 50 or 550 cells was derived. By studying minutes of meetings and through interviews, an attempt was made to ascertain whether the action taken by the committee reflected the opinions on the issue expressed by that specific local. A first attempt was made by establishing the criterion that over 50 percent of the members had to be in favor of the issue before the local committee could be expected to act—a simple application of majority rule. This limit proved too high: not a single case of nondecision was found. The decisions taken by the committees proved to be very much in agreement with the wishes of the membership. It was necessary to lower the limit to 10 percent of the members demanding action in order to obtain a few cases that might be labeled nondecisions. Specifically, we found 9 cases of nonaction in which at least 10 percent of the members had demanded action (see table 3.43); in one local this occurred on two separate issues. As can be seen from the table, four of these cases concerned nondecision in wage questions. Three of these four concerned

Table 3.43. Cases of Nondecision (questions same as comparable ones in tables 3.37 and 3.40).

Issue	Number of Cases
Higher wages	4
Working hours	3
Union activity	2
Total	9[a]

a. Nine rather than eight cases because one local showed nondecision on two separate issues.

demands from relatively small minorities for special wage benefits justified by their claim of a technically somewhat more advanced background and responsibility when compared to other groups in the local. The committee chose not to act on these demands, because it knew from earlier negotiating sessions that the central leadership would view such action as violating certain wage-political principles of conformity. In the fourth case no justification was offered by the committee for its lack of action. Three cases concerned nondecisions regarding working hours. Only in one of these cases was a clear justification given for the lack of action. In a local belonging to the Hotel and Restaurant Employees' Union the committee expressed the opinion that the requests for "more normal working hours," made by a small minority, were not possible in this type of employment; in this case the wishes of the employer had to be respected. Finally, in the area of increased union activity, one case dealt with a minority within a local of the Agricultural Workers' Union that criticized the committee for not better informing the members of the union rights of the workers, while the other case concerned a minority within a State Employees' local who wanted to see more time and effort devoted to questions related to the place of work and the resolution of conflicts between different personnel categories. In neither case was a justification for the nondecision available.

Thus, there are 8 locals with nondecisions, based on this extremely strict definition, and a total of 42 locals with decisions (see table 3.44). Apparently, nondecision is rare within the Swedish labor union movement. Theoretically, it would be possible to have cases of nondecision in all 550 cells, but they appeared in only 9, even after an extremely restrictive operationalization. From the point of view of democratic theory it would have been more reasonable to expect a limit of 50 percent, but with such a limit, not a single case of nondecision would have been found. Based on a membership opinion of 50 percent, the committees had taken action in every single case and, without exception, the action reflected the expressed wishes of the membership.

The theory of nondecision is thus irrelevant to the Swedish trade union movement, and the demand for making the union a fighting organization

Table 3.44. Decision and Nondecision.

Decision or Nondecision	Number of Locals
Locals characterized by decision	42
Locals characterized by nondecision	8
Total	50

is an empty phrase. The polemicists who advocate this are forced to
abandon the democratic notion that decisions made by the committee
should bo based on the wishes of the membership and instead assume
that the leadership should work for the "objective" interests of the workers' movement, true to the Leninist organizational principle of the revolutionary vanguard, whether the members approve or not (see, for
example, the alternative answers "nationalization of banks and large industry" and "the people should take over the means of production" in
table 3.37). The leadership of the Swedish trade unions, if it were to es-
pouse such a program, would lose most of its representativity of opinion,
today possibly its greatest democratic asset.

Authority

The final value of democracy in the model is authority. According to the
principle of interactive democracy, the leadership should be able to exe-
cute its decisions in an authoritative manner, that is, the decisions should
be acceptable to the members. The local decisions that attract the most
membership interest are those made in connection with contract negotiations and their local application. Most membership protests directed
against the union leadership in the form of wildcat strikes are effected by
these issues (phenomenon 29).

Unauthorized strikes may be a protest against both the central agreement and its local application. In both cases, they are generally directed
against the local leadership because it almost invariably supports the
central agreement. In conflict situations such as these, the local leadership can be said to lack authority: it has been unable to present its arguments in such a way that the members have been convinced that the
committee has acted in their best interest.

According to the theory advanced, conflict might arise between the
two values of democracy, authority and demands. Members either should
be critical and constitute a driving force or should accept the decisions
made by the leadership without protest. In making this operational, the
acceptance of the way the leadership executes its decisions must be qualified by membership dissatisfaction. This is done in figure 3.3, where data
concerning wildcat strikes have been compared and contrasted with data
concerning union dissatisfaction. The leadership could count on the support of 94 percent of the members. Either these members claimed not to
have noticed any strikes or any other forms of protest action at their
place of work, or else these strikes had the support of the union
leadership.

Figure 3.3. Authority within the Trade Union Movement.

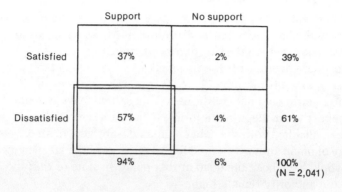

Despite the increase in unauthorized strikes during the last few years only about 6 percent of the members claimed to have noticed wildcat strikes at their place of work. Looking at the figures horizontally, one finds the figures from table 3.39 pertaining to union dissatisfaction: 39 percent were of the opinion that the union managed to extract maximum concessions from the employer during the bargaining session preceding the fieldwork, whereas 61 percent were of the opposite view. According to this definition, a leadership is said to be authoritative if, despite dissatisfaction within the union the members have been persuaded that decisions of the leadership should be accepted, and therefore refrain from unauthorized strike action. The lower left square shows this form of government to be dominant within the Swedish trade union movement,[19] whereas the lower right square indicates a form of government that is ineffective in the eyes of the members: the leadership is ill equipped to represent membership interests, and strikes are common. This form of government is rare. Even more uncommon is the form encountered in the top right square, a satisfied but frequently protesting membership. The explanation for this paradoxical phenomenon is that the protests are directed, not against the result of the agreement, which is satisfactory, but against the way the local is governed. To these few members the leadership appears to be illegitimate. Together with the other data pertaining to legitimacy, according to which an overwhelming majority expressed some form of criticism of union elections, it is possible to conclude that only a very small percentage of the members were prepared to translate their critical attitudes into action by protesting the presumed lack of democratic legitimacy of the committee.

Finally, what name shall be given to the form of government encountered in the top left square of figure 3.3? A relatively large proportion of the membership belongs here—37 percent. Locals with this form of government combine two perfectly compatible attitudes: expression of satisfaction with the agreement and profession of ignorance of any strike actions. The term utilitarian, borrowed from Etzioni,[20] best describes that form of government: the members find the union extremely useful because it extracts maximum benefits from the employer. However, the utilitarian form does not constitute a democratic ideal any more than do the ineffective or illegitimate forms. If the data concerning strikes had not been qualified with the data on union dissatisfaction, an exaggerated picture of union authority would have been drawn; the satisfied membership would have been included at that point. In spite of this, the values for union authority remain high.

The District Branch Reform

What is the attitude of members and leadership toward the district branch reform (phenomenon 31), primarily an aspect of the independent variable "organizational structure"? Table 3.45 indicates the attitudes to some statements in this area from all four union levels (the sample is limited to those with personal experience of district branches).

Table 3.45. Attitudes toward District Branch Reform: Agreement (N = Total number; M = Members; S = Section committee members; L = Local committee members; C = Central committee members).

Attitude	M	S	L	C
The district branch reform has meant better contact with the membership for the new section committees than was the case with the old locals.	33% (N = 574)	35% (N = 55)	41% (N = 85)	57% (N = 163)
Membership influence has decreased through the reorganization.	73 (N = 630)	71 (N = 55)	36 (N = 84)	24 (N = 162)
The reorganization has made the membership more critical toward the trade union movement.	77 (N = 604)	82 (N = 54)	64 (N = 84)	48 (N = 164)
The negotiations run more smoothly after the reorganization.	58 (N = 475)	82 (N = 51)	83 (N = 82)	86 (N = 153)
Communication between the national union and the local/locals has improved since the reorganization.	51 (N = 483)	64 (N = 53)	71 (N = 82)	90 (N = 165)

Note: The questions were asked only of those who had direct personal experience of the district branch reform.

Immediately recognizable in this table is the familiar picture of continuously ascending or descending series of numbers spread over the four levels with only a few minor exceptions; opinions, to a large extent, were developed along hierarchical lines within the unions. There is little evidence in this material to support the claim that the section committees are in closer touch with the membership than the local committees of old. It is true that the figures in support of this statement rise throughout the committee levels, but only at the central level did a majority support this notion. The figures reflecting reaction to the statement that membership influence has decreased through the reorganization show the reverse trend: the lower levels agreed, while the upper disagreed. A similar tendency may be found for the statement that reorganization has made the members more critical of the trade union movement. The lower levels thought that this was the case, but not until the central level did less than a majority agree. One advantage of the district branch reform is that the negotiations now run more smoothly than before. This statement was supported by a majority at all levels—least at the membership level, most strongly at the central level. The same situation exists concerning communication between the local, or locals, and the national union after the reform. A slight majority of the members found that communication had improved; at the central level the figure rises to 90 percent.

Thus, the district branch reform was viewed more favorably by the leadership than by the members, who thought that they had better communication with the committee in the old locals and that their influence had decreased. They also had become more critical of the trade union movement. The leadership was less convinced that this was the case, and strongly agreed that the negotiations now run more smoothly and that the communication between the national union and the locals had improved.

4

Variations in the Form of
Trade Union Government

Functional Testing of the Model

This study is based on the interactive democracy model, a normative model that gives a general idea of how an organization should be governed in order to be labeled democratic. Using the empirical material of the study, this model can be tested functionally. The approach planned here is to test the theoretical assumptions against the background of political reality: the different local unions will be scored according to how well they have realized their democratic objectives. The difference between such a quantitative score and the qualitative analysis of ideas encountered in chapter 1 is basically only a question of precision. In both cases, the researcher is forced to make a series of decisions concerning definitions of variables, operationalizations, and the weight to be accorded different values of democracy.

In this chapter, the trade union data will be broken down into our 50 locals. Then a scoring system will be used to show how the form of government varies from one local to another and how these variations in their turn can be related to certain institutional, economic, and social conditions.

The exact distribution of points awarded the various democratic values was in no way self-evident at the outset, but is the result of a series of experiments, arranged as usual with regard to both the theoretical significance of the concepts and the ability to distinguish empirically among different locals. Then the correlation among the three variables of the model—opinion-formation, consensus-building, and authority—is tested statistically. The fourth dichotomous variable, decision-nondecision, will be introduced more tentatively later. The basic question for testing the model is this: Is the Swedish trade union movement governed along the principles of the model of interactive democracy?

113

The point of departure for the scoring system is as follows: every member, sectional committee member, and local committee member is thought to make a number of contributions, positive or negative, to the democratic process in his or her local. Thus, the function of government, not the democratic spirit of the individuals, is described; as emphasized in discussing the method of selection used in this inquiry, it is the local unions that are the main objects of this inquiry, not individuals. An attempt is made to explain and analyze the government of these collectives, not the behavior of the individual members.

Immediately, the greatest problem in the method of scoring is encountered: Should the contributions of the members, sectional, and local leaders be accorded the same weight? Is the behavior of an ordinary member as important to the democratic interaction between membership and leadership as the behavior of an official? This is a different way of phrasing the classic democratic elite problem, an illustration of the similarity between the tasks of idea analysis and scoring. Consequently, that depends on which model of democracy is used. It would be fascinating to rewrite the history of political ideas into modern analytical science while trying to determine what weight different political theorists would have accorded the elites relative to the people. It would probably become apparent that many thinkers tried to hide their positions behind a screen of verbiage. But if theories are to be put to work, and not just become objects of historical interest, it is necessary to find that which is hidden, and develop further that which is only hinted at.

Finally, it was decided to accord twice the weight to the officials as to the members. An orthodox Rousseauist would find no difference in importance between the two. The other theorists—Weber, Michels, and Lenin—would have weighted the officials even higher, for to them the elites were much more important. To Schumpeter, whose interest was centered on the competitive quality of the elites, and to the supporters of the representational model of democracy with their interest in consensus, the elites assume a relatively greater importance than they do in the model of interactive democracy. The decision to accord officials twice the weight of members may be considered a subjective one. Why not weight it one or three instead? It would be even worse to ignore the weighting problem by according the same weight to members and leadership, in practice actually a Rousseauist position. Based on a comparison on this issue with other democratic models and after careful considerations and experiments, a weighting was used that would mirror as accurately as possible the assumptions made in the model of interactive democracy. In addition, experiments according the leadership the weight of 1.5 or 3 affect only to a very slight degree the final classification of the locals according to their governance form.

Many locals have two levels of local leadership, section and local committees. In order to avoid a problem, one single leadership level was created for each local at which section officials received half the weight of the committee members representing the union local. Then, the newly created committee level was weighted against the membership, giving the committee members the weight of two and the ordinary members the weight of one.

A schematic account shows the governing principles for calculating the scores for the answers provided by leaders and members to the questionnaire.[1] Beginning with the variable "opinion-formation" (table 4.1), the maximum number of points that an individual can contribute is ten for each of the democratic values "activity," "competence," and "system orientation." In the case of system orientation, for technical reasons, it is more expedient to measure democratic shortcomings and to use a negative score for such deficiencies, while activity and competence are given positive scores; these three democratic values are given the same weight.

At the membership level, a member who had attended a union meeting during the past twelve months contributed two points to the democratic development of the local; if he had attended three or more meetings, or contributed to the discussion at the meeting he received another point. If he had discussed union matters with a section or local committee member in the four weeks prior to the interview, he contributed one point. If he had participated in a study circle, by far the most exclusive activity value and one of the more important tools for schooling the membership, he added another four points. Should he have read most of the union periodical, he contributed one point.

The point distribution between the three questions that measured members' competence by testing their knowledge on union issues was rather even. The correct answer to the most difficult question, the law containing the nonstrike agreement, added four points instead of three. The highest possible total was ten.

In the case of system orientation, a member who entered the trade union movement from a sense of conformism or compulsion contributed one minus point. In discussing further the scoring method for this democratic value, it is important to remember the aggregate level with which the study dealt; it was not primarily the individual member who was evaluated, but the way the leadership functioned. Thus, the local received two minus points if the respondent had noticed instances of harassment directed against workers who did not belong to the union, even if

Table 4.1. The Variable "Opinion-Formation": Scoring.

Value	Score (points)
Members	
Activity	
Attended union meeting	2
Attended union meeting three times or more	1
Contributed to discussion	1
Discussed union matters with committee member	1
Participated in course or study circle	4
Read most of union periodical	1
Total	10
Competence	
Able to name union president	3
Familiar with paragraph 32	3
Able to name law containing nonstrike agreement	4
Total	10
System Orientation	
Reason for joining: conformism or compulsion	−1
Noticed harassment	−2
Acts of persecution by members or leaders	−1
Respondent collectively affiliated despite nonsocialist or Communist sympathies	−2
"The system of representation should be abolished"	−1
"Collective affiliation is an acceptable form of party membership"	−1
"Top leadership is characterized by bossism"	−0.5
"The representatives are too influential"	−0.5
"The leadership does not inspire trust in its handling of union matters"	−0.5
"The leadership does not take the views of the individual worker sufficiently into account"	−0.5
Total	−10
Leaders	
Activity	
Time devoted to union work	1.25 / 2.50 } One alternative
Discussion of union matters with members	1.25 / 2.50 } One alternative
Participated in course or study circle	2.50
Provided information	2.50
Total	10

Table 4.1 (*continued*)

Value	Score (points)	
Competence		
Number of members recognized by respondent	1 2 3	} One alternative
Understanding of agreement text	1 3	} One alternative
Acquaintance with membership opinion (local committee members only)	1 2 3 4	} One alternative
Total	10	
System Orientation		
Reason for candidacy	−2 −1	} One alternative
"Collective affiliation is an acceptable form of party membership"	−2	
"Opposition to increased membership activity"	−2	
"Low union activity is not a serious problem"	−2	
"Top leadership is characterized by bossism"	−2	
Total	−10	

the respondent was not directly involved. If these incidents had been especially serious acts of persecution by members or leaders, an additional minus point was given. If a union member had been collectively affiliated with the Social Democratic Party despite sympathies with a non-socialist party, Kristen demokratisk samling [KDS, Christian Democratic Union], or the Communists, and the right of disclaimer thus had been ineffective, two minus points were awarded. Those members who wanted to abolish the system of representation with negotiations, representatives, and various leadership levels on which the trade union movement is founded, contributed one minus point. For those who considered collective affiliation a proper form of membership in a political party still another minus point was added. Each of the following membership attitudes was given half a minus point: (1) the top leadership is characterized by bossism; (2) the representatives are too influential when compared to ordinary members and elected committee members; (3) the local leadership does not handle issues in a way that inspires confidence; and (4) the local leadership does not sufficiently consider the views of the individual worker.

The second half of table 4.1 presents the scoring method for the leadership level based on similar theoretical and empirical considerations. In the case of time devoted to union-related matters, the time spent both during and after working hours was accounted for. Different combinations contributed 0, 1.25, or 2.50 points. Further, the percentage of members with whom the leadership had discussed union issues was calculated. In this case, too, a member of the leadership was able to contribute 0, 1.25, or 2.50 points to the democratic development of the local. Participation by the leadership in a study circle is important, although not as exclusive an activity as in the case of a member; 2.50 points were given instead of 4. If the official had provided information concerning union issues at a meeting, at the work place, or at another union meeting, he also contributed 2.50 points.

Points for competence were distributed on a continuous scale from 0 to 3 depending on what percentage of the local or section members the official in question was able to recognize. Similarly, points were awarded on a continuous scale, according to how well the committee member understood the text of the agreement. The last measure of competence referred to how well acquainted the local officials were with membership opinion on six given issues (the investigation was set up in such a way that the section leadership could not be included on this question). Some 0 to 4 points were allotted on a continuous scale, depending on the ability of the committee members to gauge membership opinion.[2]

In the system orientation of the leaders, a negative score was given for any reason other than "idealism" as the motivating force behind their candidacy for the committee. System orientation among leaders was judged more severely than in the case of the rank and file. Thus, officials agreeing with the principle of collective affiliation received two minus points, as they did in each of the following three attitudes: opposition to increased membership activity if this would limit the ability of elected officials and representatives to act; unwillingness to admit that the low activity level constitutes one of the most serious problems facing the trade union movement; and the opinion that the top officials are bosses.

Table 4.2 illustrates the scoring method for the variable "consensus-building" for both the membership and the leadership. The first value, legitimacy, is applicable only to the membership. Those members who were not critical of committee elections contributed 3 points.

The second value, agreement of opinion, could yield a maximum of 20 points, amounting to half of the total possible for the variable. The view that the leadership should represent the interests of the rank and file constitutes an extremely important democratic value for the model of

Table 4.2. The Variable "Consensus-Building": Scoring.

Value	Score (points)
Members	
Legitimacy	
Not critical of committee elections	3
Members and leaders	
Agreement of Opinion	
Priority issues	10
Union objective	4
Support for low-income earners	2
Wage demands—resulting industrial failures	2
Collective affiliation	2
Total	20
Members	
Demands	
Union dissatisfaction	2
Class society	1
Total	3
Leaders	
Demands	
Ability to gauge membership dissatisfaction (local leaders)	2
Source of dissatisfaction elsewhere (local leaders)	1
Total	3
Members	
Schooling	
Social welfare benefits	1
Immigrants	1
Support for low-income earners	1
Wage demands—resulting industrial failures	1
Total	4
Leaders	
Schooling	
Social welfare benefits	1
Immigrants	1
Support for low-income earners	1
Wage demands—resulting industrial failures	1
Conception of leadership	3
Total	7

interactive democracy. Here individual points could not be awarded. The local was scored as a whole:[3] the index value for agreement of opinion for each local was based on a statistical computation of consensus between members and leaders and expressed in points. In computing this index, agreement of opinion in five areas was used. In the first question, the respondents, members as well as officials, were asked what were priority issues demanding the attention of the local. Because this is an open-ended question, it is difficult to arrive at the same answer for both members and leaders; nevertheless it is fundamentally important and may therefore yield up to 10 points (on a continuous scale, proportional to the index value for consensus). Question number two for the variable "agreement of opinion" dealt with what the union ought to work for. Because it was possible to choose from several answers, it was easier to represent opinion. The maximum score was 4 (on a continuous scale from 0 to 4, proportional to the index value for agreement of opinion). To the next three questions the answers were limited to "agree" or "disagree," which made them easier to represent, and each yielded a maximum of 2 points on a continuous scale.

The third value, demands, consists at the membership level of dissatisfaction with the agreement and 2 points were allotted. In addition, 1 point was given for the opinion that Sweden is still a class society, because both members and, to a lesser extent, leaders expressed dissatisfaction with society in such radical terms. The leaders were limited to local committee members only. They contributed up to 2 points, on a continuous scale, if they were able to gauge correctly the dissatisfaction of the members. If the source of dissatisfaction in their opinion was to be found not with the local (section/representative/members) but elsewhere (employer/LO/the state), 1 point was awarded; dissatisfaction of local origin ought actually to result in minus points, which was not possible for technical reasons.

In the case of the value "schooling," a member earned 1 point for each of the attitudes expressed toward social welfare benefits, immigrants, and the two aspects of the wage policy of solidarity. This applied to the leaders as well. However, 3 points were added for those committee members who have evidenced leadership qualities by agreeing that the leadership is not always obliged to represent exactly the interests of the membership, but that it is often more important to oppose any reactionary tendencies among the rank and file. The 3 points for conception of leadership were matched at the membership level by 3 points for legitimacy, so that mathematical symmetry between the two levels also exists within the variable "consensus-building."

However, the number of respondents varied from one local to another;

a handful of small locals, containing only some 10 members, constituted an especially noticeable deviation. The ability of a local to achieve a high score was thus dependent on the total number of contributing members of that local. In order to avoid a situation in which locals with a large number of members and committee members were apt to appear more highly developed in a democratic sense, the following operation was done. After computing the local score for each of the democratic values, a new computation was made of the score, expressing it as a percentage of the maximum score possible for the local. In this way, percentage scores representing the variables "opinion-formation" and "consensus" were calculated for all the locals. These figures may be compared independently of the size of the local.

The third variable on which the model was tested is authority. Authority was measured by relating union dissatisfaction to the occurrence of unauthorized strikes. Then, a percentage figure for each local was calculated in the same way as authority was measured for the trade union movement as a whole. Through these calculations a percentage score was obtained, reflecting the degree of democratic development within the various locals in the areas of opinion-formation, consensus, and authority.

To further clarify the scoring method, it is necessary to use a concrete example of the score of an individual local.

Table 4.3 illustrates the breakdown of the score for the variable "opinion-formation" for Local 1. Category (1) shows the points earned for the local. Members contributed 115 points for activity, 120 for competence, and −109 for system orientation; the corresponding score for local and sectional officials reflecting the democratic values of activity, competence, and system orientation is indicated. Category (2) shows the consolidation of local and sectional committees, weighted 2 and 1 respectively, to one single committee level; the membership level was not included in this step. Category (3) expresses the score as a percentage of the maximum score possible for each of the three democratic values for both levels; here the leadership scores higher than the membership in activity and competence; the leadership is more democratic. This is generally true of the locals of the study. Category (4) reveals the consolidation of the membership and leadership levels, weighted 1 and 2 respectively, into a single level. Category (5) shows the percentage figures for the three democratic values for the local after the consolidation into a single level. Category (6) indicates the total after adding the figures for the three democratic values. Thus, Local 1 achieved a percentage score of 56 for the variable "opinion-formation."

Table 4.4 shows a similar breakdown of the score for the variable

Table 4.3. Opinion-Formation in Local 1: Scoring (A = Activity; C = Competence; S = System orientation).

Category	Membership			Local Committee			Section Committee		
	A	C	S	A	C	S	A	C	S
(1) Points earned	115	120	−109	45	34	−16	56	49	−39
(2) Consolidation to one single committee level								weight 1	
(3) Percentage points of maximum possible (two levels)	24	25	−23	52	53	−25			
		weight 1			weight 2				
(4) Consolidation to one single level	39	41	−24						
			56						
(5) Percentage points of maximum possible (one level)									
(6) Total score based on weight system of table 4.1. Percentage points of maximum possible									

Table 4.4. Consensus-Building in Local 1: Scoring (L = Legitimacy; A = Agreement of opinion; D = Demands; S = Schooling).

Category	Membership				Local Committee				Section Committee			
	L	A	D	S	L	A	D	S	L	A	D	S
(1) Points earned	39		103	83	–		14	43	–	–		62
(2) Consolidation to one single level	L	A	D	S	→ 15				weight 2	weight 1		
(3) Percentage points of maximum possible (two levels)	L	A	D	S	L	A	D	S				
	28		73	44	–		64	76				
(4) Consolidation to one single level					→ 75					weight 1	weight 2	
(5) Percentage points of maximum possible (one level)	L	A	D	S								
	28	75	67	65								
(6) Total score based on weight system of table 4.2. Percentage points of maximum possible	67											

"consensus-building" for Local 1. Category (1) shows the points earned by the local. The membership contributed 39 points for legitimacy; committee members were excluded at this point. In the case of "agreement of opinion," there is no individual score, only a score for the local as a whole, proportional to the index value assumed by "agreement of opinion." The local received 15 out of 20 points possible for this democratic value, a figure expressed later in the table as 75 percent of the possible maximum score. Only members and local committee members contributed points for demands. All three levels received points for schooling.

Category (2) indicates the consolidation of local and section committee members, weighted 2 and 1 respectively, into a single committee level; the membership level was not included here. Category (3) shows the score as a percentage of the total possible for each of the democratic values. Category (4) merges the membership and committee levels, weighted 1 and 2 respectively, into a single level. Category (5) indicates the percentages for the four democratic values after the consolidation of the local into one level. "Agreement of opinion," with 75 percent, achieved the highest score among the democratic values. Category (6) indicates the total score after adding the percentage figures for the individual values. Local 1 achieved a score of 67 percent for the variable "consensus-building."

Calculation of the third variable, authority, for Local 1 is illustrated in figure 4.1. After qualifying the data relating to wildcat strikes with data on union dissatisfaction, the 47 answers obtained from the members of this local were translated to reflect a score of 62 percent for the variable "authority" within the local. Local 1 presents comparatively high scores for the three variables; it is one of the better locals. Interaction between

Figure 4.1. Calculation of Authority in Local 1.

	Support	No support
Satisfied	30%	2%
Dissatisfied	62%	6%

100%
(N = 47)

members and leaders in this local functions in such a way as to fulfill reasonable demands for an interactive democracy.

What is meant by "reasonable demands"? What are the normative criteria for satisfactory opinion-formation, consensus, and authority? A certain minimum point score was needed to constitute a normative criterion in the form of a percentage figure for each of the three variables, a figure that the local then had to surpass in order to be judged acceptable. Because the variable "authority" is based on a single computation, it is harder to determine what is reasonable, and it thus becomes more arbitrary. A minimum limit of 50 percent of the possible score for this variable was considered acceptable for a local.

Because minus points were also given out for the variable of opinion-formation, it was more difficult to reach a high percentage figure for this variable than for the other two. The normative criterion should therefore be set lower than 50 percent in this case. Thus, what might constitute "reasonable demands" for each individual point had to be considered. To meet this requirement, a member should have attended one union meeting, but not three or more; nor was it necessary that he participated verbally. He should have spoken with a committee member about union matters during the four weeks prior to the interview, and he should have read the greater part of the union periodical, but he need not have attended a study circle. For the competence value, a total of 6 points was needed—a correct answer for the two easy questions, but not for the more difficult. Similar considerations were made in the case of system orientation. These judgments of what might be considered reasonable led to minimum values that might be attained through other combinations than those mentioned (for example, it might be possible to speak at a meeting instead of reading the greater part of the union publication). Opinion-formation in a local was considered acceptable if it reached a minimum score of 40 percent.

Similarly, a reasonable limit for consensus-building has been established point by point. The absence of minus points means that the normative criterion could be set somewhat higher. A normative criterion of 60 percent of the total score possible was required for the level of consensus to be judged acceptable.

The normative criteria for the variables opinion-formation, consensus, and authority, respectively, are 40, 60, and 50 percent. Local 1 reached 56, 67, and 62 percent and is, according to the definitions, a democratic local.

Figure 4.2 attempts to show how the percentage scores vary among the 50 locals for the three variables. Each column spans an interval of 5 percent. The lowest value for opinion-formation in any local is 11.7

Figure 4.2. Variation among Locals with regard to Opinion-Formation, Consensus, and Authority.

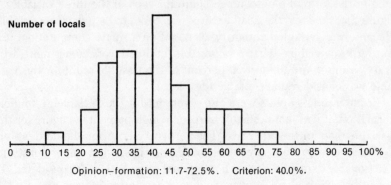

Opinion–formation: 11.7-72.5%.   Criterion: 40.0%.

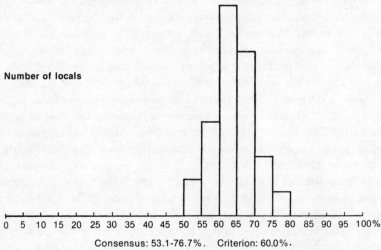

Consensus: 53.1-76.7%.   Criterion: 60.0%.

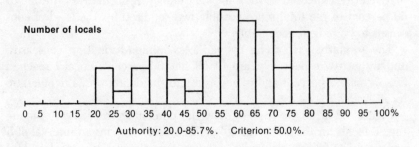

Authority: 20.0-85.7%.   Criterion: 50.0%.

percent of the total possible, the highest is 72.5 percent (computations included one decimal not reflected in the table). Consensus is remarkably concentrated and well developed: the lowest value for any local is 53.1 percent, and the highest 76.7 percent. Authority is more evenly distributed—at a somewhat lower level, but still quite high. The spread ranges from a low of 20.0 percent to a high of 85.7 percent.

How are these three variables related? Are they interrelated, as the model of interactive democracy assumed; that is, does high opinion-formation lead to high consensus and high authority, and low opinion-formation to low consensus and low authority?

The model of interactive democracy has been tested against actual conditions in the unions in figure 4.3. Each variable has been divided into

Figure 4.3. Model Testing.

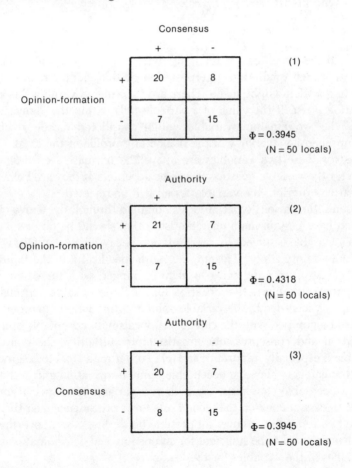

Consensus

	+	−	
+	20	8	(1)
−	7	15	

Opinion-formation

$\Phi = 0.3945$
(N = 50 locals)

Authority

	+	−	
+	21	7	(2)
−	7	15	

Opinion-formation

$\Phi = 0.4318$
(N = 50 locals)

Authority

	+	−	
+	20	7	(3)
−	8	15	

Consensus

$\Phi = 0.3945$
(N = 50 locals)

locals above (+) and below (−) the normative criterion for the variable in question, and correlative computations have been made. The normative criterion was not used to establish an automatic cutoff point. It would have been too stringent a measure; it would be hard to say for example that a figure of 40.1 percent for opinion-formation would be acceptable, while 39.6 percent would not. In order to show greater sensitivity to the material, an "uncertainty zone" of 10 percent of the spread for each variable around the normative criterion was calculated:

$$\text{for opinion-formation } \frac{(72.5 - 11.7) \times 10}{100} = \pm 3.0 \text{ percent;}$$

$$\text{for consensus } \frac{(76.7 - 53.1) \times 10}{100} = \pm 1.2 \text{ percent; and}$$

$$\text{for authority } \frac{(85.7 - 20.0) \times 10}{100} = \pm 3.3 \text{ percent.}$$

Should the value for a variable fall within the "uncertainty zone," a more thorough qualitative interpretation of the characteristics of the local in question will be made. There are two rules governing this interpretation. First, if the value of a variable falls within the "uncertainty zone," the two remaining variables will be considered in order to obtain a comprehensive overview of the democratic profile of the local. If the values for these two variables are above the normative criterion, the value for the variable questioned will be accepted. If they are below the normative criterion, the variable tested will be rejected.

Second, the various types of locals obtained through the above classification have certain main characteristics that should be observed even when a variable is subject to interpretation because its value falls within the "uncertainty zone." This applies more specifically in the following three cases: (a) in order for a local to be ranged with the category of locals above the normative criterion for all three variables, special importance is accorded to the variable opinion-formation; (b) in order for a local to be grouped with the category of locals with acceptable opinion-formation and consensus, but unsatisfactory authority, the consensus variable is especially important; and (c) in order for a local to be grouped with the category showing acceptable opinion-formation and authority, but unacceptable consensus, the authority variable is of special importance. In case of conflict, the second rule takes precedence over the first. These two rules do not cover all possible borderline cases; nevertheless, they have proved to be sufficient for an unequivocal determination of all the values of the variables for the locals.

Figure 4.3 indicates the existence of positive correlations among the variables, as postulated in the model of interactive democracy; all three figures show more locals concentrated in the top left square (+ for both variables) or the bottom right square (− for both variables). However, there are several instances of other combinations. The precise testing has been done by computing the phi coefficients resulting in the correlative measurements indicated by the figure. In all three cases, the correlation has been confirmed statistically at the 1 percent level through a chi^2 test.

More specifically, 26 percent of the locals tested are governed according to the specifications of the model of interactive democracy, with high percentage figures for all three variables. This means that only one out of every four trade union locals functions, according to this study, in a democratically satisfactory manner. Thirty percent of the locals are so passive that they can be said to lack any democratic features.

Both these types of locals—the 26 percent democratic locals and the 30 percent passive locals—can be said to confirm the model: if a high degree of interaction between members and leaders exists in the process of opinion-formation, then consensus-building and authority too will be high and vice versa; if opinion-formation is low, so are consensus-building and authority. This appeared in the testing of the model as positive, albeit far from perfect, correlations among the three variables opinion-formation, consensus-building, and authority. However, it was also shown that there exist other intermediate unanticipated forms, which deserve closer scrutiny.

Classification

The model of interactive democracy has up to this point served as a framework for the systematic analysis of interaction between members and leadership within the Swedish trade union movement. Through the testing of the model, the correlation among the constituent variables has been established, and while a large part of the locals function according to the hypothesis of the model, there also exist intermediate forms. The testing of the model does provide a basis for classification of the 50 locals into a number of categories representing various forms of union government.

Three variables, each with two variable values—above and below the normative criterion—may be arranged in eight logically possible combinations. Three of these forms, the single-variable cases, turn out not to contain any locals: acceptable opinion-formation alone, acceptable consensus alone, and acceptable authority alone.[4] The remaining five possi-

bilities will form the five types of locals in the classification outline presented in figure 4.4. The illustration in the uppermost square will be recognized as the model of interactive democracy with a complete set of variables. The other four squares lack one or more variables, the ones for which the type of local shows unacceptable values. The uppermost square thus contains the democratic locals. Thirteen of the 50 locals (26 percent) belong in this category.

In the lowermost square are those locals which were referred to as passive. They are characterized by values below the normative criterion for all three variables. Fifteen of the 50 locals (30 percent) belong here.

The three intermediate forms remain. The left square at the middle level contains what are called the impotent locals. These are characterized by values above the normative criterion for the opinion-formation and consensus-building variables, but below the normative criterion for authority. Despite the high degree of consensus which has been devel-

Figure 4.4. Classification of Sample Locals.

oped within these locals, they are unable to achieve results (for example, in local wage negotiations) that are acceptable to the membership. Seven of the 50 locals (14 percent) belong in this category.

The square on the far right of the middle level contains what are called the therapeutic locals. They are constructed analogously to the impotent locals and are characterized by values above the normative criterion for opinion-formation and authority, but below the normative criterion for consensus-building. Even though the local displays considerable activity, competence, and system orientation in the process of opinion-formation, it is still not able to develop consensus. Decisions made by the committee are not questioned by the membership, however, and are accepted without strikes. Membership participation in the process of opinion-formation thus becomes ineffective; this participation might be referred to as therapeutic. Eight of the 50 locals (16 percent) belong in this category.

The center square of the classification figure contains what are called the manipulative locals. These are characterized by values below the normative criterion for the variable "opinion-formation." Nevertheless they display a high degree of consensus-building and authority. Despite a lack of participation and knowledge of union matters by the members, they still declare themselves satisfied with the way the committee handles union questions and accept committee decisions without resorting to strike action. Seven of the 50 locals (14 percent) belong here.

Finally, a correlation will be made between this classification and the results of the discussion of decision-nondecision, the fourth variable of the model. This correlation will be extremely tentative. Simply, how are the eight locals in which a tendency to nondecision might be discerned distributed over the five classes of locals? The results indicate (see table 4.5) that the majority, as might be expected, belong among the passive

Table 4.5. Decision-Nondecision and Classification of Locals.

Category	Locals with Nondecision
Democratic	0
Impotent	0
Manipulative	1
Therapeutic	2
Passive	5
Total	8

locals, and none among the democratic. The manipulative category contains one, and the therapeutic two.

Explanation

The analysis of the various ways in which the unions are governed has now reached the stage where a final classification of the 50 locals has become possible. They have been divided into five categories referred to as democratic, impotent, manipulative, therapeutic, and passive. This concludes in principle the analysis of the dependent variable (democracy) of the study. Now it is necessary to explain the variations in union governance by correlating the classification of the locals with the seven independent variables. What makes a local impotent or therapeutic? Does a high wage level within a local lead to a democratic or perhaps a passive form of government? What are the effects of mobility and the number of immigrants on the democratic process? How are the Communist, as opposed to the Social Democratic, locals distributed over the five categories?

Organizational Structure

The correlation between organizational structure and the form of government can be seen in figure 4.5. The 50 locals have been broken down according to the three values of this variable: (1) district branches with representational bodies; (2) district branches without representational bodies; and (3) smaller locals. Each value of this variable has been given a classification figure, each local has been assigned a place in it, and percentage figures have been calculated.

The results of this analysis proved surprising: the proportion of democratic locals is demonstrably lower (13 percent) among district branches with representational bodies than in the two other forms of organization (33 percent and 31 percent). Representational bodies were introduced to safeguard certain democratic values during the transition to larger units, the district branches. Something quite unforeseen and less desirable has taken place. It was noted earlier that the general membership was considerably more critical of the district branch reform than was the leadership at the higher levels. The members maintained that contact with officials was better in the old locals, that they had less influence now, and that the rank and file had become more critical of the trade union movement. Somewhat less passivity existed in district branches with represen-

Figure 4.5. Organizational Structure and Form of Government. Sums are not always 100 percent because of rounding to whole numbers.

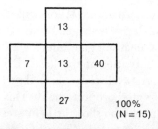

(1) District branches with representational bodies

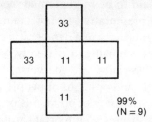

(2) District branches without representational bodies

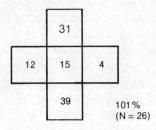

(3) Smaller locals

tational bodies than in the smaller locals. But instead of leading to an ideally functioning democracy the increased interaction between members and leadership had, to a considerable degree, veered toward a therapeutic form of government (40 percent as compared to 11 percent and 4 percent, respectively, for the two other forms). The analysis of data shows that no other factor contributes more to the explanation of the therapeutic form of government than does the existence of representational bodies.[5]

These findings were so surprising that, in order to gain more insight into the phenomenon, a selective analysis of the district branches with representational bodies in the sample was undertaken. Members and committee members at the local and sectional levels in all fifteen of these district branches were asked how representational bodies and the committees functioned. Representational bodies were introduced in these locals primarily as a means of guaranteeing all membership groups a fair influence over the activities of the local. Different categories, such as men/women, immigrants/Swedes, and above all, different trades and sections were represented proportionally. This often entailed persuading members to participate who show little interest in union matters. Group affiliation rather than interest in the activities of the local was often the deciding factor in the election. The foremost function of the representational body can be said to be to guarantee social representativity.

However, social representativity is not a democratic value in itself. On the contrary, representativity in a democratic context refers to representativity of opinion. A woman can perfectly well represent men, immigrants can represent Swedes, or vice versa, and a certain person can represent the interests and opinions of people in occupations other than his own. That representativity of opinion is possible also between different social groups constitutes an important principle of the theory of liberal democracy. This does not mean that the experience that members of the representational bodies and committee members gain directly on the job is of no consequence to union democracy. A local committee often takes up very concrete problems such as workers' protection and the working environment; on these issues a representative from the affected group might be an asset. But democracy requires that the views of the representative be anchored in the membership through opinion-formation and consensus-building; otherwise, there is a risk that they reflect only the opinions of the representative, no matter how strictly the exact representation of the various categories has been observed. To no one's surprise the district branches with representational bodies showed very little agreement of opinion. Thus, many of them are found in the therapeutic square of figure 4.5 because these locals lack genuine consensus-building: legitimacy, demands, schooling, and, above all, agreement of opinion were inadequately developed.

The lack of consensus found in the district branches with representational bodies may also be analyzed in a different manner. The most important issue by far for opinion-formation and consensus-building within the trade union movement is the wage policy of solidarity. The data indicate that the support for a wage policy of solidarity was decidedly weaker in district branches with representational bodies, characterized by an underdeveloped public spirit.[6]

Nevertheless, this does not necessarily mean that representation works counter to union democracy. Representational bodies were often introduced as part of the district branch reform. Even if no data are available, it is possible to guess what kind of local chose this system of representation and what kind did not. Those locals that had problems with internal democracy under the old system might now introduce representational bodies in order to strengthen membership influence, while those that had not had these problems might not feel the need for representation. Thus, the decline in democracy need not have been caused by representation. Indeed, it might have been worse without the representational bodies: the locals might have been passive instead of therapeutic. The therapeutic form of government is at least a kind of midway point on the road to democracy. A practical recommendation could be made after the analysis of the correlation between organizational structure and the governance form of the union: the branches should try to improve the building of consensus, rather than experiment with different systems in order to guarantee absolute social justice among various categories. For example, this could be done through study circles dealing with the wage policy of solidarity as the goal of the democratic endeavors of the trade union movement. Democracy primarily implies decision making in the interests of the people, and the content of these decisions must be a vital part of the decision-making process. Otherwise there is a real risk that the decision-making process will not be carried forward by factual-content motives, but might ultimately be turned into a therapy for formalists.[7]

Wages

There is a more direct correlation between wages and form of union government (figure 4.6): the higher the wage level, the more developed the democracy (53 percent, 21 percent, and 6 percent for high-wage, medium-wage, and low-wage occupations, respectively). The proportion of passive locals increased correspondingly from the two groups with a higher level of wages and very little internal difference as to passivity (13 percent and 16 percent, respectively) to the lowest wage group (63 percent). High wages thus lead to a democratic form of government, low wages to passivity.

In reviewing the union-related phenomena that were to be taken up for discussion in this study, two specific questions were raised concerning the relationship between wages and union policy. The first deals with the wage level and the attitude toward a wage policy of solidarity: Is the strongest support for this policy to be found among the low-income earners who have the most to gain from it, and what is the attitude of the

Figure 4.6. Wages and Form of Government. Sums are not always 100 percent because of rounding to whole numbers.

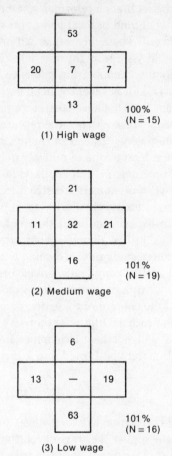

(1) High wage   100% (N = 15)

(2) Medium wage 101% (N = 19)

(3) Low wage   101% (N = 16)

high-income earners? The second question concerns the wage level and wildcat strikes. There are differing theories about who has initiated the recent unauthorized strikes. Is it the high-income earners who in this way protest the limitations imposed by the wage policy of solidarity on possible wage increases, or is it still the traditionally disadvantaged, the low-income earners, who strike?

The data, after dividing the 50 locals by wage level and public spirit, showed that the support for a wage policy of solidarity was not especially strong among the low-income earners.[8] On the contrary, the group that was the most lukewarm toward the wage policy of solidarity was composed primarily of low-income earners! Also, after dividing the locals by wage level and frequency of wildcat strikes, the data showed that unauthorized strikes became more frequent the lower the wage level of the local. The notion that what we see now is primarily a new type of strike—the protest of the high-wage earners against solidarity—can thus be dismissed.[9]

The wage variable thus indicated locals that in many respects appeared close to the ideal. The democratic form of government was more highly developed in high-wage locals, where there was strong support for a wage policy of solidarity and lower frequency of wildcat strikes.

Sociotechnical Conditions

The pattern is less clear when the classification figure was analyzed according to the three values of the variable "sociotechnical conditions" (figure 4.7). There is very little difference in the democratic form of government. However, the passive form of government decreases from light to heavy work, and the manipulative form of government increases in locals with heavy work.

Two separate phenomena may be discerned. On the one hand, there is the nature of work and the work environment. Heavy work constitutes an obstacle to a democratic form of government. The opinion-formation variable and especially membership activity assume low values in locals with heavy work. On the other hand, the sociotechnical variable seems to mirror a cultural phenomenon, which might be called the traditions of the workers' movement. The locals with the heaviest work belong to those unions that traditionally were in the forefront of the labor struggle—the miners, metal workers, paper workers, forest and wood workers. While these locals show low scores for opinion-formation, especially activity, they achieve very high scores of consensus, especially agreement of opinion and schooling.

Thus, the traditions of the workers' movement are more alive in the locals involving heavy work. These locals school their members more effectively in the ideology of union solidarity, and their leaders are more representative of membership opinion. But the heavy work leaves the members little energy for active participation in union matters with the result that they express their confidence in the leadership without participating or informing themselves of the issues. The form of government for locals with heavy work tends to be manipulative. The analysis of data shows that heavy work is the largest contributing factor to the manipulative form of union government (to be shown in table 4.6).

Figure 4.7. Sociotechnical Conditions and Form of Government.

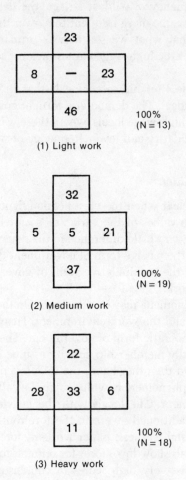

(1) Light work

(2) Medium work

(3) Heavy work

However, this interpretation is less certain than, for instance, the analysis of the consequences of the wage variable and several of the following analyses. From a scientific point of view, it would have been more satisfactory to have different indicators for the nature of the work and union traditions, so that these phenomena could have been kept separate for analytical purposes.

The technical development of the future, which reduces heavy work for these men at the very heart of the union movement, should make it possible for the trade union movement to increase their membership activity and to counteract the tendency toward a manipulative form of government. But this can be done only if the trade union movement manages to compete successfully for the leisure time and interests of the industrial workers.

Mobility

The pattern of the wage variable emerges once more in an analysis of the classification figure according to the variable "mobility" (figure 4.8). Democracy improves with a low turnover (70 percent, 27 percent, 12 percent, and 0 percent for locals with low mobility, medium mobility, high mobility, and high mobility with immigrants, respectively), and passivity increases with a high turnover (20 percent, 7 percent, 47 percent, and 50 percent for the same groups, respectively). Seventy percent of locals with a low mobility rate have a democratic form of government— an extremely high figure, second highest in this study. The special group consisting of locals with a large number of immigrants has the lowest

Figure 4.8. Mobility and Form of Government. Sums are not always 100 percent because of rounding to whole numbers.

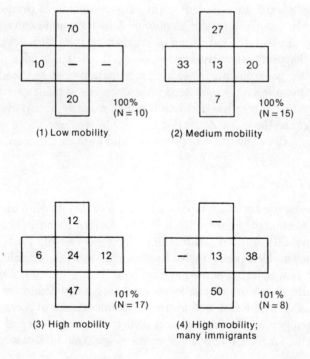

democratic score. Here there are no democratic or impotent locals; the largest portion is made up of passive locals, followed by the therapeutic. Thus, locals that function in a democratically sound manner are characterized by a stable membership body with a low annual turnover. It is ironic that one of the possible effects of the attainment of a "more mobile society"—a stated Social Democratic objective on the economic and labor market front, though less vigorously pursued today than during the progressive 1960s—might be a weakening of union democracy through an increase in mobility.

Sex

Are women characterized by apathy in politics and union affairs, as is often maintained? The division of the locals into three groups according to sex distribution (figure 4.9) indicates that women are apathetic. The passive form of union government increases along with the proportion of women (21 percent, 33 percent, and 43 percent, respectively) and the proportion of democratic locals decreases (33 percent, 25 percent, and 14 percent).

In addition to this main picture emerging from figure 4.9, there is a tendency toward an impotent form of government in predominantly male locals—good interaction in opinion-formation and consensus, but a certain propensity for indicating dissatisfaction through wildcat strikes. Among the predominantly female locals, there is a tendency toward therapeutic government, in which participation does not lead to consensus. Nevertheless, women accept the decisions of the leadership without protest. It is possible that one result of a partly new pattern of sex roles might be the union activation of women—to put a sociological perspective on the correlation between sex and form of union government.

Length of Membership

In analyzing the correlation between length of membership and form of union government (figure 4.10) the same pattern found in the cases of wages, mobility, and sex is discernible: long membership leads to better democracy and less passivity. No single square in all the classification figures can show as high a percentage figure as the one indicating the democratic form of government in locals with long membership tenures—73 percent. Every official is well aware of the importance of recruiting new union members while they are still young. The probability of finding a democratic form of union government is greatest in locals with high

Figure 4.9. Sex and Form of Government.

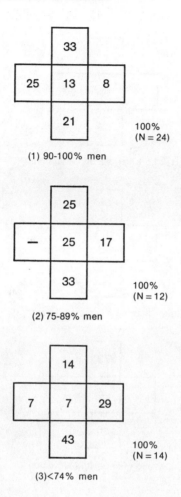

(1) 90-100% men

(2) 75-89% men

(3)<74% men

wages, low mobility, a large proportion of men, and long average membership tenure.

Political Party Preferences

Finally, the classification figure has been analyzed by Social Democratic and Communist locals (figure 4.11). Communist locals are more active than the Social Democratic. Among the Communist locals there is not a single passive one. However, this activity has not led to a satisfactorily functioning democratic form of government. In most of these locals

Figure 4.10. Length of Membership and Form of Government. Sums are not always 100 percent because of rounding to whole numbers.

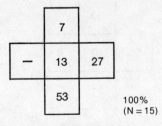

(1) Short membership affiliation

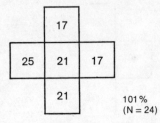

(2) Medium membership affiliation

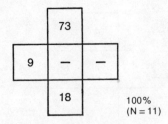

(3) Long membership affiliation

intensive interaction between members and leaders exists in opinion-formation and consensus-building. At the same time, frequent membership protests are directed against the way in which the committee handles such union issues as local agreements. The largest percentage of the Communist locals is represented by the impotent form of government. The question that was asked earlier regarding the connection between Communist party sympathies and wildcat strikes thus has to be answered in the affirmative. Unauthorized strikes are more frequent in Communist locals than in Social Democratic.

Figure 4.11. Political Party Preferences and Form of Government. Sums are not always 100 percent because of rounding to whole numbers.

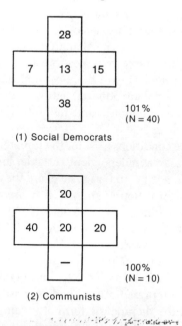

(1) Social Democrats

(2) Communists

With the help of the seven independent variables the variations in the ways the unions are governed have been explained. Even if clear patterns emerge for the majority of the variables, there is uncertainty in this kind of analysis. Before being able to break down the classification figure according to independent variables, it was necessary to refine a large number of positions, judgments, and decisions both about the interpretation of where in the figure individual locals belonged, and about where the limits of the values of the independent variables should be drawn. The slightest adjustments of these positions or limits could have resulted in a partly different picture of the variations in the form of government. To attempt to extract more than an outline of the main tendencies from the material or make more far-reaching pronouncements might mean endowing with exaggerated importance facts that might simply be the expression of random variations in the material.

Requisite Conditions

Having broken down the classification figure, variable by variable, it is possible to see how important the seven independent variables are to the five categories of locals.[10] This will result in yet another characteristic of the five forms of government and their requisite conditions.

The coefficients listed in table 4.6 describe the influence of the explanatory variables, taking into account their partial overlap, while the preceding analysis is based on a calculation of each explanatory variable separately. From this table it is possible to determine that length of membership and wage level are the most important factors for a democratic form of government: long affiliation and a high level of wages. Party sympathies (Communist) and mobility (low) are also relatively important.

Similar requisite conditions exist for the impotent form of government, although in this case the independent variables are less important. Here, too, length of membership and wage level are the crucial factors; to some extent organizational structure and mobility are also significant.

The manipulative form of government has one requisite condition, one which yields the highest coefficient of the table. This is the sociotechnical condition of heavy work.

The therapeutic form of government, too, is characterized by one condition of overriding importance. This is organizational structure: district branches with representational bodies constitute the richest ground for the growth of the therapeutic form of union government.

The requisite conditions for the passive form of government are similar to those for the democratic, except the variable values are reversed: short membership affiliation, low wages, and high mobility top the list for this form of government.

Prediction

When social scientists test their theories against empirical reality, they are basically dealing with prognoses or predictions.[11] By manipulating data in a quasi-experimental fashion, they seek to predict what reality would look like if the data or the known conditions were altered in a certain way.

By calculating the correlation between the dependent classification figure and the seven independent variables, information concerning the requisite conditions for the various forms of union government was obtained. If, with the aid of a computer this information were used to obtain a prognosis on the expected location in the classification figure for each of the 50 locals, a comparison could be made between such a prediction and the actual distribution, thus measuring the predictive power of the explanation. Such an operation was performed. The results are indicated in table 4.7.

Table 4.6. The Five Forms of Government: Requisites and Beta Coefficients (O = Organizational structure; W = Wages; ST = Sociotechnical conditions; M = Mobility; S = Sex; Me = Length of membership; P = Political party sympathies).

Democratic		Impotent		Manipulative		Therapeutic		Passive	
Me	0.2648	Me	0.1789	ST	0.2724	O	0.2111	Me	0.1627
W	0.2354	W	0.1442	W	0.1348	ST	0.1091	W	0.1604
P	0.1777	O	0.1269	S	0.1077	Me	0.1066	M	0.1435
M	0.1348	M	0.1189	M	0.0543	M	0.0718	O	0.1071
O	0.0451	P	0.0825	O	0.0465	W	0.0403	S	0.0729
S	0.0403	ST	0.0489	P	0.0371	S	0.0231	ST	0.0544
ST	0.0014	S	0.0332	Me	0.0085	P	0.0006	P	0.0036

The most important figure in this table is multivariate theta. This constitutes a measurement of the predictive power of the explanation. A multivariate theta of 80 percent was calculated.

The actual distribution is indicated to the far right of every row in the classification matrix, while the results of the prognosis are listed at the bottom of each column. The first row of the matrix shows that 11 of the 13 (84.6 percent) democratic locals have been correctly predicted. One

Table 4.7. The Fifty Locals by Form of Government: Prediction and Actual Distribution.

Multivariate statistics

Multivariate theta	0.8000				
Correctly classed wt. N	11	5	5	5	14
Correctly classed proportion	0.8462	0.7143	0.7143	0.6250	0.9333

Classification matrix

Actual	Predicted					
	Democratic	Impotent	Manipulative	Therapeutic	Passive	Total
Democratic	11	0	1	0	1	13
Percent	84.62	0.0	7.69	0.0	7.69	
Impotent	1	5	0	0	1	7
Percent	14.29	71.43	0.0	0.0	14.29	
Manipulative	1	1	5	0	0	7
Percent	14.29	14.29	71.43	0.0	0.0	
Therapeutic	0	0	0	5	3	8
Percent	0.0	0.0	0.0	62.50	37.50	
Passive	0	0	0	1	14	15
Percent	0.0	0.0	0.0	6.67	93.33	
Total	13	6	6	6	19	50

democratic local was incorrectly attributed to the manipulative form and one to the passive.

The second row of the matrix indicates that 5 of the 7 (71.4 percent) impotent locals were correctly classified. One impotent local was classified with the democratic form of government, one with the passive.

The third row indicates that 5 out of 7 (71.4 percent) manipulative locals were correctly classified. One had been incorrectly grouped with the democratic form of government, one with the impotent form.

Row four shows that 5 of the 8 (62.5 percent) therapeutic locals were correctly predicted, the least accurate result. Three locals were here attributed to the passive form of government.[12]

The fifth row indicates that 14 of 15 (93.3 percent) passive locals were correctly classified. The prognosis overestimated somewhat the number of passive locals (19 instead of 15), underestimated the number of cases belonging to the three middle forms, and correctly estimated the number of democratic locals.

Multivariate theta simply indicates the number of locals on the diagonal, from the upper-left to the lower-right cell, that were correctly classified. This proved to be 40 of 50 locals (80 percent). In order to determine the explanatory power expressed by this value a comparison should be made with the result of a random distribution. Based on the marginal distributions given, a random distribution is calculated: $13^2/50 + 7^2/50 + 7^2/50 + 8^2/50 + 15^2/50 = 11$ locals in the main diagonal, a multivariate theta of 22 percent. To determine whether the explanation of the variation in the form of government with the aid of our seven independent variables is successful, this figure should be compared to 80 percent.

Measure of Effect

Figure 4.12 presents a schematic setup of this study, with the computed effect for each independent variable mentioned in chapter 2 included. There are now eight rather than seven squares. The eighth, dotted square measures how much of the variation in the form of government could not be explained by the seven independent variables: 20 percent of the variation (one minus multivariate theta $[1.00 - 0.80 = 0.20]$). The sum of the effect of the variables is greater than 1.00 because of a certain overlap in the explanation.

The difference in the internal effects of the variables is relatively insignificant. It is possible to distinguish a group of three variables with especially pronounced effect on the form of union government: the variables

Figure 4.12. Influence of Independent Variables on the Dependent Variables: Bivariate Theta (O = organizational structure; W = wages; ST = sociotechnical conditions; M = mobility; S = sex; Me = length of membership; P = political party preferences).

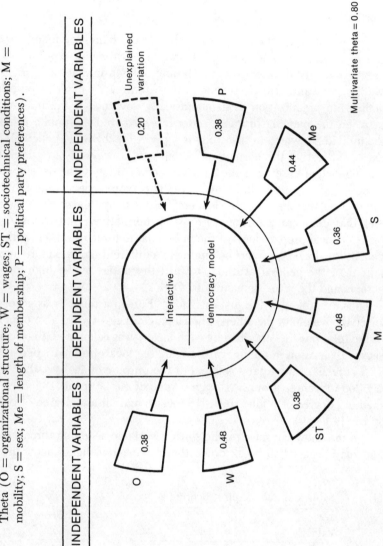

of wages and mobility, each with a theta of 48 percent, and length of membership, with a theta of 44 percent. The four remaining variables have a somewhat lower effect.

Normative Testing of the Model

The descriptive level detailed the behavior of committee members and the rank and file, and functional analyses distinguished some fundamental patterns of democracy, including opinion-formation, consensus-building, and authority. In setting forth the normative model, a postulate defined an organization as democratically governed if the interaction between the membership and leadership furthered the public spirit of the individual, which in this study is support for the wage policy of solidarity. In testing the normative model, it was necessary to establish a scoring system to serve as the basis for a description of the development of public spirit in the different locals. This score reflects only the attitudes of the members, not the leaders, for it is the public spirit of the former that democracy furthers. From the normative point of view, the psychological preparedness of the individual to forego a raise in order to benefit low-income earners belonging to a different union is more important than the general attitudes toward the duties of the high-income earners and the wage demands of LO.

Thus, in table 4.8, the first question, "Forego a raise," was accorded twice the weight of the others. Then a percentage—the number of points of the total possible obtained by each local—was calculated. Figure 4.13 shows a variation in public spirit among the locals from 34.7 percent to 72.5 percent of the total possible. For the purpose of analysis, they were divided into three groups: (1) high degree of public spirit (18 locals); (2) medium degree of public spirit (18 locals); and (3) low degree of public spirit (14 locals).

We may now consider public spirit a variable assuming three values, and may proceed to break down the classification figure according to

Table 4.8. Public Spirit: Scoring.

Value	Score (points)
Forego a raise	10
Support for the low-income earners	5
Wage demands—resulting industrial failures	5
Total	20

Figure 4.13. Variation in Public Spirit among Locals.

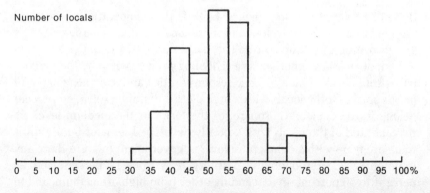

Public spirit: 34.7-72.5%

Figure 4.14. Public Spirit and Form of Government. Sums are not always 100 percent because of rounding to whole numbers.

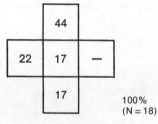

100%
(N = 18)

(1) High public spirit

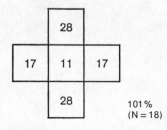

101%
(N = 18)

(2) Medium public spirit

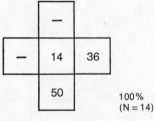

100%
(N = 14)

(3) Low public spirit

these three variable values (figure 4.14). Is the democratic form of government more highly developed in those locals that are characterized by a high degree of public spirit? The basic normative hypothesis is confirmed: democracy functions as a schooling process whereby the individual is trained to assume greater responsibilities and a higher degree of public spirit. Of the locals with a high degree of public spirit, 44 percent belong in the democratic square; of the locals at the medium level, 28 percent; and of the locals with a poorly developed sense of public spirit there are none with a democratic form of government (nor are there any impotent).[13] Correspondingly, passivity rises from 17 percent and 28 percent to 50 percent, in descending order from high, to medium, and to low values on the scale for public spirit. The test lends powerful support to our view of democracy based on the philosophy of John Stuart Mill. Democracy is not only a goal, it is also a means. Democracy not only represents certain values such as public spirit and solidarity, it also indicates a way to achieve this goal: through participation in the decision-making process the public spirit of the individual is developed.

5

Democracy within the
Trade Union Movement

What may be expected from democracy? What motivates people to work for a democratic form of government? What values does the Swedish trade union movement hope to attain through a well-functioning democracy? The answers to these questions have remained virtually unchanged through the decades. The views propounded in the debate on the problems of trade union democracy may easily be traced back to classical arguments first formulated at the turn of the century by the pioneers and earliest critics of the union movement.

The main historical ideas that have served as the background and necessary condition for the fieldwork of this study point to two fundamentally different views of democracy. According to one, democracy constitutes a method for the rapid realization of that which is good. The class society of the nineteenth century, divided into a ruling elite and a politically powerless and economically proletarianized working class, would be replaced by a classless society, governed according to the principle of one man–one vote and characterized by economic and social equality. This would be achieved through rapid and far-reaching constitutional reforms, or possibly even through revolution. These great expectations were followed by bitter disappointment, and when Robert Michels, the pioneer of trade union research, proved not only that there existed an elite within the trade union movement—the very movement that was to prepare the way for the classless society of socialism—but also that the rise of an oligarchy was inevitable in all organizations, it was a shocking discovery to many of the impatient idealists who had perceived democracy as a way of rapidly realizing a just society.

Some then deserted the fundamental view of democracy and espoused the politics of Lenin for the purpose of establishing a counterelite, in whose hands all power would be concentrated for as long as it took to liquidate the remnants of the predemocratic society. Half a century later, this time has not yet arrived for the Leninists, for in those systems where they are in power they have never been observed to hand over the power that they once seized by force. The Leninists' repeated claim that their power monopoly is a transitory thing appears less and less credible as the years pass by.

Others maintained that the difficulties arose from not pursuing the egalitarian ideals forcefully enough. They advocated more faithful adherence to the recommendations of Rousseau by refraining from electing any leaders at all and seeking to involve everybody equally in the decision-making process. The result was organizations totally lacking in power. The experiments in this direction within the Swedish trade union movement toward the end of World War I were short-lived. The recent reappearance of Rousseauists—as participants in mass meetings and revolutionaries within, as well as outside, the universities—was also brief. The disappointments of half a century ago resulted primarily in a more urgently felt need for leaders; it also led to the adulation of charismatic leaders and to the transformation of egalitarian populism into fascism. Robert Michels eventually supported Mussolini, probably because he was a disappointed Rousseauist.

According to another opinion, democracy is not a way to realize rapidly that which is good, but rather a way to avoid as far as possible that which is bad. The proponents of this view are in no way opposed to the equalization of social classes or to social reforms, but they do not expect rapid changes, for they know that these require an organization that in effect will reestablish an oligarchy. In order to avoid this evil, they advocate an arrangement whereby the necessary leaders, the inevitable elites, are checked through regularly held elections. Here, political theory has usually seized on the definition of the principles of democracy suggested by Joseph Schumpeter, who had in turn been inspired by Weber: the risks of an oligarchy can be avoided if there are several elites competing with one another for power. The difficulty with this definition is that it neither mentions the active participation by the individual citizen in the political process—one of the cornerstones of the classic democratic doctrine—nor does it take into account faulty election procedures. In some cases, routinely made nominations or diffuse cleavages between the candidates may make systems without competing elites appear more legitimate than competitive systems in the eyes of the membership. The latter situation exists within the Swedish trade union movement between locals with and without contested elections.

A more recent definition, well represented within Swedish political science research, is based on a political technique different from competition: democracy is thought to be realized to the extent that there exists agreement of opinion between the elected and the electors. One difficulty with this definition is that it fails to indicate how the opinion-formation process of the leadership is to take place. Influence and agitation must necessarily imply that a certain discrepancy of opinion between leaders and electors is tolerated, so that the leadership does not merely passively reflect temporary majority opinions.

Despite these objections, the most outstanding characteristics of the stable democracies of Western Europe and the United States are a multiparty system, competition, and government by representative opinion. Political theory in this part of the world has left the area of moral philosophy and tends more and more toward pure organizational theory.

One view of democracy comments upon economic, social, and moral conditions; another view is limited to a discussion of the technique of the act of governing. One is a definition based on reality; the other a formal definition of democracy. One view supports a socialist democracy; the other a liberal democracy. This is not merely an academic distinction; it is reflected in world politics.

However, one theme has been neglected within the field of the political history of ideas, and it tends to get lost in the battle between the two main philosophies just described. Those who work within the framework of this philosophy seem curiously unaware or ignorant of its tradition. It is the democratic schooling program of John Stuart Mill, the main thesis of which has often been summarized within this book: such a degree of interaction should exist between leaders and members within a democratic organization that the public spirit of the individual is furthered. The proponents of the representational model limit themselves to a technical aspect of Mill's work when they speak of democracy as representation of opinion. According to Mill, one purpose of democracy is to widen the horizons of the individual, increase his willingness to assume responsibility, and lift his moral and intellectual life to a higher plane— all this through individual political participation. The Swedish democracy, with its special traditions of popular movements, has to a high degree been marked by this program of democratic schooling. "You wear your Sunday best at committee meetings"—this view has helped educate Swedish citizens to democratic responsibility in political parties, unions, educational organizations, temperance unions, rent associations, and so forth.

Is this a realistic expectation of democracy? Is it reasonable to expect democracy to develop the public spirit of the individual? This question warrants further clarification. The term public spirit as it relates to con-

ditions within the trade union movement has been defined, for the purposes of this study, as encompassing a wage policy of solidarity. The
interpretation here has been rendered difficult because this policy has
seldom been discussed from an ideological-political point of view. Those
tendencies within LO that during the last few years have found their expression in the principles of a wage policy of solidarity can best be characterized from a historical point of view as opinion-formation in the
spirit of John Stuart Mill designed to further the public spirit of the
members as well as their sense of responsibility to include also economically less privileged groups.

The trade union movement has generally been successful in creating a
climate of opinion in favor of a wage policy of solidarity. This study indicates that almost half of the members are prepared to forego a raise if
this would benefit low-income earners belonging to other unions. Three-
fourths of the membership think that it is right that LO supports low-income earners even if this means that other groups will be put at a disad-
vantage. However, the economic consequences of a hard-line wage
policy find only limited support among the members. At the committee
levels, there is more widespread support for all of the elements of a wage
policy of solidarity than there is among the members.

Is there anything to indicate that the members have acquired this positive attitude through participation in unions? Has democracy and nothing else given rise to public spirit? Might not low-income earners
demand solidarity out of pure group interest?

In order to answer these questions, it is necessary to define the concept
of democracy. The subject of this study has been the definitions of those
phenomena and processes that are necessary and desirable in a democracy and the way in which the Swedish trade union movement has
sought to realize them. In dividing the 50 locals into three groups, depending on whether the public spirit of the members was high, medium,
or low, locals defined as democratic constituted 44 percent of the total in
the high group, 28 percent in the medium group, and 0 percent in the
low group. The passive locals, by this definition, constituted 17 percent,
28 percent, and 50 percent, respectively, of the three groups. Thus, there
is a strong correlation between public spirit and a democratic form of
government. The data further indicate that the support for the wage policy of solidarity is rather weak among the low-income earners. The low-
wage groups are the least receptive to the idea of a wage policy of solidarity! This paradoxical situation can be explained. The democratic
processes are more highly developed within the high-wage locals of LO
than within the low-wage locals. The high-income earners develop

stronger support for a wage policy of solidarity through union-related studies and other forms of opinion-formation than the more passive and less schooled low-income earners, who would be the main beneficiaries of such a policy. Democracy therefore functions as a schooling process through which the public spirit of the individual is developed.

Thus, democracy fosters better individuals with a more highly developed sense of solidarity. But this is a long-term opinion-formation process that cannot be accelerated. A classless society can be introduced by peaceful means only after the political and legal arguments in favor of such an equalization have become firmly entrenched among the citizens.

The concept of democracy has been outlined in the model of interactive democracy. The purpose of the democratic form of government is the development of the public spirit of the individual through a process of interaction between leaders and members. Two levels were specifically included in the system: leadership and membership. Interactive democracy is thus not a direct but an indirect democracy, in which decisions are made by the leaders after opinion-formation among the members and not through mass meetings or other direct democratic methods. The acceptance of a leadership has been brought about because public spirit—here defined as the attitude toward the wage policy of solidarity—is in all respects more highly developed among the leadership than among the members. The development of this attitude takes place through active agitation and schooling by the leaders; this is not a spontaneous grass-roots development. Another reason for the acceptance of leaders is the classic objection to the Rousseauist point of view: without a strong central leadership an organization is unable to work for its goals in an effective manner.

The interaction between members and leaders in an interactive democracy takes place primarily during the opinion-formation process. The Swedish trade union movement encounters many problems in this area. The union-related activities and the factual knowledge of the members are relatively limited, without being strikingly low: 4 out of 10 members attended union meetings, of those less than half participated verbally, a little more than a quarter discussed union matters with the leadership during a given month, approximately the same number regularly read most of the union periodical, 1 out of 10 participated in study circles or similar activities, only a quarter were able to name their union presidents, half of them knew the contents of Paragraph 32, and very few were aware that the provisions concerning a nonstrike agreement were set forth in the Collective Bargaining Law. The activity level and competence of the leaders are higher, although their knowledge of membership opinion is sometimes colored by wishful thinking as well as a tendency to ascribe to the membership the same opinions as they themselves hold.

The most serious aspect of opinion-formation and of union democracy in general is the lack of respect for free opinion-formation as expressed in the collective affiliation of union locals with the Social Democratic Party. This is not a popular practice; 64 percent of the members find this form of party membership wrong. Even among the section and local leadership a majority opposed collective affiliation, and only at the central level, on the steering committees of the national unions and on the General Council, is this form of membership favored. The problem is mainly that the so-called right of disclaimer with which the Social Democrats defend the existing order has proved of little value. Only 5 percent of the members in the collectively affiliated locals took advantage of the right of disclaimer. Of the members who did not exercise this right 18 percent sympathized with the non-socialist parties or the Communists; if the undecided or those who have not indicated their party sympathies were included, a full third of the members would not be Social Democrats. Concerning how those workers are treated who prefer to remain outside the trade union movement, 21 percent of the members said that they had noticed harassment directed against the outsiders in the form of "snide remarks and verbal pressure," but even more seriously "anonymous letters," "threatened beatings," "verbal abuse and violent actions," and sanctions by the leadership.

All this adds up to a rather dark picture of the respect for minority rights within the Swedish trade union movement. The leadership perceives that influencing membership opinion is one of its primary duties and that a broad base of support for union ideology is an important objective for the movement. In the case of the wage policy of solidarity, they have often been successful. Nevertheless, in the process of influencing opinion, excessively harsh methods are sometimes used. Interactive democracy presumes that the leadership is able to maintain a balance between an active influencing of opinion and a respect for the rights of the minority. This balance has not always been maintained within the Swedish trade union movement.

The next step in the process is consensus-building; the interaction between leaders and members in an interactive democracy is supposed to lead to consensus regarding the guidelines for action of the trade union movement. In this case, reality is close to the ideal. For both the leaders at different levels and the members agreed upon the objectives of the unions. With a difference of only a few percent, leaders and members generally made the same demands: a better working environment, increased wages, better job security, and shorter working hours.

Certain differences of opinion obviously exist between members and leaders. Nationalization of various kinds was more often favored by the leaders than by the members: approximately half of the leaders urged socialization, as compared to about a quarter of the membership. Many members favored a price and wage freeze. This stand is directly opposed to the official program of the union movement, and it is remarkable that as many as three-quarters of the members made this demand; as might be expected the percentage in favor of this alternative decreases at the higher levels of the union hierarchy. The differences concerning the wage policy of solidarity and collective affiliation have already been discussed. There was very strong support for the former, with the exception of some of its economic aspects, already at the membership level; this support increased at the higher levels. The latter issue encountered a certain resistance that was not transformed into majority acceptance until the central committee level.

Nevertheless, a high degree of agreement of opinion remains the dominant impression. The response rates on various issues were compared at the various levels statistically, while trying to pinpoint the degree of agreement by means of Robinson's Index, ranging from 0.00 (no agreement of opinion) to 1.00 (perfect agreement). Apart from the above-mentioned questions—the economic consequences of a wage policy of solidarity and the lack of representativity among the central committee members on the issue of collective affiliation—the results indicated a high degree of agreement; in most cases the index values fell between 0.80 and 0.95.

When seen against this background the criticism leveled against union leaders in the mass media—that the leaders consist of "bosses" unrepresentative of membership opinion—appears oddly unjustified and uninformed. At no point is an attack against the Swedish trade union movement less justified than when it criticizes the union leaders for not being representative of opinion.

Interactive democracy stipulates representativity of opinion, but not that the leaders be socially representative. On the contrary, it is important to a democratic view that different social groups be able to engage in a mutual exchange of opinion, influence each other, and represent each other in various organizations. Nevertheless, the social background of the union leaders is of some interest. The occupation of the father seems unimportant to a career within the union movement; about the same proportion (50 percent) of the leaders as of the members had their roots among industrial workers, but it is very important whether the father belonged to the union movement and voted for the Social Democrats. This was increasingly true at the higher levels of the hierarchy. With regard to the political background, and thus returning from the question of social representativity to representativity of opinion, it was found that the Social Democrats were heavily overrepresented at the committee levels. Approximately 70 percent of the union members preferred the Social Democratic Party, with the Center Party in second place with 10 percent, and the Communists in third with 8 percent. This compares with a figure of 90 percent of the local committee members and of 98 percent at the central level in favor of the Social Democrats. These figures support the image of a trade union movement ruled by a strongly ideologically conscious leadership prepared to agitate vigorously for its view of society.

Agreement of opinion is not static in an interactive democracy. It is the result of the interaction between the members and the leadership. It is the task of the members during the consensus-building process to make demands; the task of the leadership is to school the members in union ideology. In both cases, the data are indicative of great vitality. In spite of the positive wage development for the Swedish industrial worker, most members have not shown a conservative complacency but urged the leaders with radical demands to advance the position of the movement. The leaders have proved successful in their schooling effort and have shown a strong sense of leadership, as when they declared that it was sometimes their duty to oppose the reactionary tendencies that might be found among the workers.

The third process within union democracy is the exercise of authority. The decisions mutually agreed on by leaders and members in an interactive democracy have to be applied in an authoritative manner, and they have to be accepted by the membership. A situation of conflict might at times arise between a role of passive acceptance and an active formulation of demands. Passive acceptance is not a democratic asset in and of itself, no more than absence of authority makes possible the vigorous pursuit of one's plan of action. This role conflict has been resolved in the following way. According to the specification above, union authority means that there are no wildcat strikes directed against the local leadership. Although wildcat strikes have become somewhat more frequent in Sweden of late, they are still rare by international standards. Only 6 percent of the members reported that unauthorized strikes have occurred at their place of work. The data concerning wildcat strikes have been combined with data on membership demands for better negotiated contracts.

The analysis showed that most local committees actually enjoyed a position of authority: 57 percent of the membership accepted the argument of the leaders that they could not have gone farther during contract negotiations had they wanted to. Other combinations of data on dissatisfaction and strikes are less acceptable from a democratic point of view: locals where members did not demand more than they got (37 percent of the membership) and locals with wildcat strikes where the leaders failed in their arguments in favor of the contract and thus did not secure membership acceptance (6 percent of the membership). Along with the high agreement of opinion the considerable degree of authority enjoyed by the steering committees of the unions constitutes the most highly developed democratic value of the Swedish trade union movement.

The prerequisite method for testing the model was the ability to analyze the material of the 50 locals studied in order to see which combinations of opinion-formation, consensus-building, and authority might be empirically observed in the various forms of union government, and then to study the relationship of these variations to different institutional, economic, social, and political party conditions.

A classification figure containing five different forms of union government, referred to as democratic, impotent, manipulative, therapeutic, and passive locals, was developed.

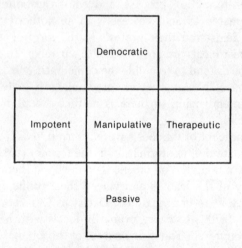

The democratic form of government accounts for 26 percent of the locals studied. This form of government is identical to the ideal, interactive democracy: a high degree of interaction exists between members and leadership during the opinion-formation process. As a result there is genuine consensus, and the decisions made by the leaders are accepted by the members and can be authoritatively executed. The democratic form of government is primarily found in locals with members of long standing, low membership turnover, high wage level, and few women.

The passive locals, the reverse of the democratic, constitute 30 percent of the locals. This form of government lacks interaction between members and leaders during the opinion-forming process, consensus is not reached, and the leadership enjoys no authority, a situation that results in numerous wildcat strikes. These locals generally possess the opposite characteristics of the democratic locals: short membership affiliation, large turnover, many immigrants, low wages, and a large number of women. Mobility within the labor market, a policy favored by the Social Democratic government, has created certain difficulties for trade union democracy.

Both the democratic and the passive forms of government confirm the hypothetical relationships of the model of interactive democracy. However, the three remaining forms of government of the classification figure were not predicted. They may be described as middle forms between the democratic and passive locals, containing only a few democratically well-developed processes. Fourteen percent of the locals were characterized by an impotent form of government: despite active interaction during the opinion-formation process, and consensus-building, the committees were unable to achieve results in an authoritative way. The members then registered their protests in the form of wildcat strikes. Many Communist locals are governed in this manner. In other respects, the impotent locals tend to resemble the democratic ones: the wage level in them was unusually high, they are predominantly male, and the average length of membership in them is neither exceptionally short nor especially long.

Another 14 percent of the locals were referred to as manipulative. In spite of inadequate opinion-formation in the form of passivity and ignorance primarily among the members, they declared themselves satisfied with the policy of the leaders and voiced their confidence for actions with which they were unacquainted. Decisions were accepted without wildcat strikes. In this category primarily locals with heavy and noisy work were encountered. The heavy nature of the job makes opinion-formation more difficult, and especially membership activity is low. On the other hand, the traditions of the workers' movement are exceptionally strong within these unions with heavy manual labor, and the leadership can count on the confidence of the members. It is too early to tell whether technological improvement will be able to remedy this situation in the future, or whether the traditions will lose their hold on the unions with heavy manual labor so that light work and the passive form of government will remain linked also in the future.

Finally, 16 percent of the locals functioned with the therapeutic form of government. In spite of great activity and intensive interaction during the opinion-formation process, these locals are unable to develop consensus. Instead, the more they talk, the more they disagree. Paradoxically, the decisions made by the leaders do not result in membership protests in the form of wildcat strikes, but are accepted. Membership participation in the opinion-formation process becomes ineffectual, and participation might be described as therapeutic. Primarily, a new type of local fell within this category: district branches with representational bodies. Representational bodies were introduced in many locals in order to protect certain democratic values during the transition to the district branch system. The large geographic areas, inadequately developed consensus-building, and a tendency to elect candidates on their social representativity rather than on the basis of their opinions have led to therapy rather than democracy, a distinction that has not always been observed in Swedish politics. Special questions put to those with direct experience of the transition to district branches with or without representational bodies revealed that the members were rather critical of these larger units, while the committee members were more positive. According to the members, contact with the leadership was better in the old locals than in the present sections and clubs. They also said that they had less influence under the present system and had become more critical of the trade union movement. The committee members at the various levels were not convinced that this was the case and stressed instead that negotiations ran more smoothly and that contact between the national unions and their locals had improved. Possibly the fact-finding committee appointed by the LO Congress of 1976 will come up with suggestions for improving union democracy within district branches with representational bodies.

Is it possible to ascribe one of five forms of government—democratic, impotent, manipulative, therapeutic, and passive—to the trade union movement as a whole? The attempts at a quantitative testing of the model of democracy for the trade union movement as a whole have not been published, for this is more suitable for cases where direct comparisons are possible. For example, it would be fascinating to compare union democracy within LO with the conditions within Tjänstemännens centralorganisation [TCO, Central Organization of Salaried Employees] and Sveriges akademikers centralorganisation [SACO, Central Organization of Swedish Professional Workers]. However, the testing of the model against one single case encounters difficulties in determining where the limits should be drawn. Minute changes in the norms might mean considerable differences in the empirical results without any gain in the understanding of union democracy and its conditions. The final answer to the question "How are the unions governed?" is therefore not quantified, and the attempt to place the form of government of the trade union movement as a whole into any one of the five squares of the classification figure has been based on a general judgment of the developmental levels and characteristics of the various democratic processes.

To begin with, it is possible to determine that the Swedish trade union movement at the overall level is not distinguished by an impotent, therapeutic, or a passive form of government. Consensus-building with such highly developed agreement of opinion is not found in the passive or therapeutic forms of government. Nor is such well-developed exercise of authority found in the passive or impotent systems.

The choice then remains between a manipulative form and a democratic form of government. Are the deficiencies found in the opinion-formation process so significant that this process fails to meet the criteria for union democracy, and must be labeled manipulative, or is the opinion-formation, in spite of its flaws, acceptable on the whole, so that the form of government deserves to be called democratic? On the one hand, the attempts at a quantitative calculation indicated that the membership and the committee members at the central level failed to reach the percentage score established as the criterion for a democratic opinion-formation process in the individual locals—40 percent of the total possible. On the other hand, it might seem unjustified and unfair to demand that the committee members at the central level be as familiar with the climate of opinion among their 1.8 million members as the local committee members are with their members, which may amount to a couple of thousand. It might be added that calculations including a middle level composed of local leadership did not alter the general picture. The form of government for the unions as a whole had probably better be labeled manipulative rather than democratic in a fully developed sense. For it is important to direct attention to the differences in democratic development that exist between the smoothly functioning consensus-building and authority, and the somewhat less highly developed opinion-formation.

The problem areas of trade union democracy in today's Sweden are largely different from those pointed out by the radical reporters and journalists who, during the early 1970s, launched a mass-media attack against the purported bossism within the Swedish trade union movement. According to the above findings, the Swedish trade union movement is not governed by an oligarchy in the form of more or less conservative bosses who fail to represent the opinions of the rank and file. On the contrary, the high degree of agreement of opinion built up within the movement constitutes one of the foremost assets of union democracy. Whatever the differences, for example, concerning nationalization, they indicate that the leaders are more radical than the members. Thus, the problem is not in the activity of the leaders, but rather in the passivity of the members. Great efforts are being made to engage the members through study circles and other educational activities. However, within the sizable organization of today's LO relatively large groups still remain untouched by these efforts, and exhibit a rather moderate level of activity and information. The problems indicated by the concept of a manipulative form of government are the direct opposite of bossism, in the sense of nonrepresentative leadership, if the distinctions inherent in the definitions are maintained. According to these, the manipulative form of government is characterized by a high agreement of opinion (and also by strong authority for the leaders), in spite of less well-developed membership activity and other phenomena related to opinion-formation. Thus, the agreement of opinion is very high despite a relatively moderate level of membership activity, little bossism is found among the leaders, and the leaders often manage to represent the members' opinion, even when this opinion is not fully articulated.

The consensus built up around trade union ideology seems to have developed through pressure from above, through manipulation by the leaders for the purpose of achieving greater support among the members for the wage policy of solidarity and other important union-related lines of action. This opinion-formation process has sometimes assumed democratically less desirable aspects because the shortcomings in the opinion-formation process are not limited to the two values referred to as activity and competence. The third value of the opinion-formation process, system orientation, presents its own problems: collective affiliation, the unused right of disclaimer, the harassment of outsiders, and the lack of freedom of opinion. Here one must not overlook the possibility of a connection with certain other processes related to the form of union government. Freedom of opinion and agreement of opinion might be mutually dependent and balanced so that the high agreement of opinion might be the partial result of pressure in the direction of the "right" way of thinking during opinion-formation. To put it bluntly: it is not difficult for leaders to be representative if there is only one view to represent. In all probability, the leaders of LO take this into account in planning their line of action, for an ideological split within the workers' movement must be avoided. Unity, a common front, and ideological conformity have given LO its strength. Nevertheless, if union democracy is to be strengthened further, better ways of guaranteeing the freedom of opinion of the individual must be found without risking a loss of the ideological community—undeniably a delicate and complicated task.

The main picture of trade union democracy emerging from this study is that of an opinion-formation process with certain flaws such as relatively moderate membership activity, limited knowledge of union matters, and, in practice, restricted freedom of opinion. However, there is good consensus-building with high agreement of opinion between members and leaders—with the exception of a few special problems in district branches with representational bodies—and a position of authority for the leaders whose actions generally have the support of the membership.

Democracy is not just a matter of form or organizational technique. Careful attention was paid to the contents of union activity and to the processes through which the leaders seek to gain membership support for this activity. That the trade union movement has been so successful in this respect may primarily be attributed to special indigenous traditions of ideas. Many foreign and Swedish observers have described uniformity in Sweden in sociological terms and have attempted to explain the successful political building of the welfare state by pointing to homogeneity of language, race, religion, and so forth. To this picture must be added the tendency to conformism in the very development of ideological and political norms in that society. The ideological propaganda of the workers' movement has been so successful in Sweden that it is today almost regarded as unseemly for a political party to question such key words in union ideology as solidarity and equalization of income. Protected by this ideological and political conformism, the Swedish trade union leadership is presently in the process of realizing John Stuart Mill's program of fostering democracy. Through intensive propaganda, union leaders are seeking to gain the members' support for the wage policy of solidarity and union ideology, and by doing so to widen the horizons and responsibilities of the members to include areas outside the sphere of self-interest. To a considerable extent this reformist action program has widespread support among the members. This is then the long and laborious road that the Swedish trade union movement has chosen toward a classless society, evidently without a second glance at the supposed shortcuts provided by the Rousseauists or Leninists—shortcuts that would ultimately increase rather than decrease the risk of oligarchy within the trade union movement and society as a whole.

Notes

1. How Should Democratic Organizations Be Governed?

1. Robert Michels, *Political Parties: A Sociological Study of the Oligarchical Tendencies of Modern Democracy*, trans. Eden and Cedar Paul, foreword Seymour Martin Lipset (New York: Free Press, 1962), pp. 342 and 365.

2. Ibid., pp. 368 and 370.

3. Ibid., p. 358.

4. Jean Jacques Rousseau, *The Social Contract*, trans. and introd. G. D. H. Cole (New York: Dutton, 1950), p. 94. The book was first published in 1762. Rousseau wrote in his book that he considered it against the order of nature that the majority ruled the minority. Democracy in the strictest sense of the word (that is, direct democracy) had never existed and would never exist.

5. C. N. Carleson, *Makt och parti i modern organisation* (Stockholm: Fram, 1918), p. 58.

6. Ibid., pp. 47–48.

7. Minutes of the Constitutional Congress of the Left Socialist Party in Stockholm, May 13–16, 1917, p. 5.

8. Carleson, *Makt och parti*, p. 19.

9. Minutes of the Constitutional Congress, pp. 64 and 83.

10. *The Theory of Social and Economic Organization*, trans. A. M. Henderson and Talcott Parsons (Glencoe, Ill.: Free Press, 1957), contains important parts of Weber's great work *Wirtschaft und Gesellschaft: Grundriss der verstehenden Soziologie* (1922).

11. Sverker Gustavsson, *Debatten om forskningen och samhället. En studie i några teoretiska inlägg under 1900-talet* (Stockholm: Almqvist & Wiksell, 1971), p. 40.

12. Carl J. Friedrich, "Some Observations on Weber's Analysis of Bureaucracy" in *Reader in Bureaucracy*, Robert K. Merton et al., eds. (Glencoe, Ill.: Free Press, 1952), p. 31.

13. See Peter M. Blau, "Critical Remarks on Weber's Theory of Authority," *American Political Science Review*, 57 (1963), p. 315.

14. V. L. Allen, *Power in Trade Unions. A Study of Their Organization in Great Britain* (London: Longmans, 1954), p. 25.

15. Ibid., p. 15.

16. *Fackföreningsrörelsen,* no. 13, 1974, p. 6.

17. It is possible to arrive at another norm of action using Weber's analysis of the concept of authority as the point of departure. Weber's thoughts on charismatic leadership gained great popularity in central Europe between the wars; the trade unions, subordinated to the dictatorship, became the building stones of a fascist apparatus of state. This fascist norm of action is of no relevance to the Sweden of today. However, it became the norm that Robert Michels finally embraced. Disappointed in socialism and democracy, he became more and more convinced of the historical inevitability of authoritarian regimes. He wrote of fascism in positive terms and accepted in 1928 a professorship offered by Mussolini.

18. V. I. Lenin, *State and Revolution* (New York: International Publishers, 1969), p. 84.

19. Lennart Berntson, "Sveriges kommunistiska parti och leninismen 1919–1929," *Arkiv för studier i arbetarrörelsens historia,* 3 (1972), pp. 14–34.

20. See Joseph A. Schumpeter, *Capitalism, Socialism, and Democracy,* 2d ed. (New York: Harper & Brothers, 1947). For criticism of the application of the theories of Hayek, see Leif Lewin, *Planhushållningsdebatten* (Stockholm: Almqvist & Wiksell, 1967), pp. 263–347. On Schumpeter, see Leif Lewin, *Folket och eliterna. En studie i modern demokratisk teori* (Stockholm: Almqvist & Wiksell, 1970).

21. On democratic theory in postwar political science, see Lewin, *Folket och eliterna,* especially pp. 92–98.

22. Seymour Martin Lipset, Martin Trow, and James Coleman, *Union Democracy. What Makes Democracy Work in Labor Unions and Other Organizations?* (Glencoe, Ill.: Free Press, 1956), p. 405.

23. Nils Elvander, "Organisationsdemokrati—en omöjlighet?" *Sylf-Nytt,* 21 (1962), no. 1, pp. 3–5.

24. For the relationship between the concepts of competition and representativity see Lewin, *Folket och eliterna,* pp. 109–47.

25. Jörgen Westerståhl, "Demokratidebatt," *Statsvetenskaplig Tidskrift,* 74 (1971), p. 373. See also his book *Ett forskningsprogram. Den kommunala självstyrelsen 1* (Stockholm: Almqvist & Wiksell, 1970), and his article "Representativ demokrati eller deltagandedemokrati," *Dagens Nyheter,* 11 January 1972; Sören Holmberg, *"Riksdagen representerar svenska folket". Empiriska studier i representativ demokrati* (Lund: Studentlitteratur, 1974), and Lars Strömberg, "Väljare och valda. En studie av den representativa demokratin i kommunerna," mimeographed (Department of Political Science, University of Gothenberg, 1974).

26. See John Stuart Mill, "Representative Government" in *American State Papers,* Great Books of the Western World, 43 (Chicago: Encyclopaedia Britannica, 1952) pp. 325–442. The work was first published in 1861.

27. Concerning limitations on those areas where the elites permit competition, see section The Functioning of Interactive Democracy on "decision" and "nondecision," below.

28. Westerståhl in *Statsvetenskaplig Tidskrift,* 24 (1971), p. 373.

29. From the static point of view, to which researchers have been limited

until now by a lack of resources, agreement of opinion is measured at a specific point in time. If the model were expanded to become dynamic, it might be possible to visualize a certain discrepancy in agreement of opinion at T_1, which in the ideal case, at T_2, would become almost perfect. This would occur after the elites had had time to devote themselves to opinion-formation and after they were influenced by grass-roots opinion.

Within the model of interactive democracy the dynamic exchange between leaders and membership is under continuous observation, and the notion that it might sometimes be the duty of a leader to go against membership opinion is specifically mentioned as a positive value.

30. Cf. my discussion of "civility" in *Folket och eliterna*, pp. 147–162.

31. Certain minor adjustments, primarily terminological in nature, have been made in the original presentation of the model of interactive democracy made in *Folket och eliterna*, p. 227 (fig. 13).

32. Lewin, *Folket och eliterna*, pp. 46, 57.

33. Ibid., pp. 138–141.

34. In *Folket och eliterna* three demands are made of the elites: "competition," "representativity," and "civility." They correspond to "legitimacy," "agreement of opinion," and "schooling" in this study.

35. Ingemar Lindblad, *Svenska kommunalarbetareförbundet 1910–1960* (Stockholm: Tiden, 1960), pp. 397–420 and 440–472.

36. See Lewin, *Planhushållningsdebatten*, pp. 407–409. A similar conclusion could have been drawn by using as a point of departure a well-known reference on systems analysis such as David Easton, *A Systems Analysis of Political Life* (New York: Wiley, 1965). Easton too uses the term "demand."

37. Leif Lewin, *Statskunskapen, ideologierna och den politiska verkligheten* (Stockholm: Rabén & Sjögren, 1972), pp. 24–26.

38. See Peter Bachrach and Morton S. Baratz, "Two Faces of Power," *American Political Science Review*, 56 (1962), pp. 947–952.

39. Peter Bachrach and Morton S. Baratz, "Decisions and Non-decisions: An Analytical Framework," *American Political Science Review*, 57 (1963), pp. 632–642. The concepts "decision" and "non-decision" were discussed in *Folket och eliterna*, pp. 127–134.

2. The Governance of Swedish Trade Unions

1. This chapter contains thirty-seven separate terms followed by a number 1–37 in parentheses. They indicate the phenomena related to union government that will be studied. The remaining sections of this chapter will discuss these terms in detail; they will be interpreted within the framework of the model of interactive democracy and will become the dependent and independent variables of this study. Cf. figure 2.3, table 2.12, and figure 2.4.

The development of the organizational structure of the Swedish trade union movement is the subject of a special study by one of the doctoral candidates assisting in this project, Axel Hadenius. For an in-depth study of this area see his doctoral dissertation *Facklig organisationsutveckling. En studie av Landsorganisationen i Sverige* (Stockholm: Rabén & Sjögren, 1976).

2. Sidney and Beatrice Webb, *Industrial Democracy* (London: Longmans and Green, 1920), pp. 3–21.

3. Jörgen Westerståhl, *Svensk fackföreningsrörelse. Organisationsproblem, versamhetsformer, förhållande till staten* (Stockholm: Tiden, 1945), pp. 84–85.

4. *Fackföreningsrörelsen och näringslivet* (Stockholm: Tiden, 1941), p. 215; Minutes of the LO Congress, 1941.

5. Axel Hadenius, "Integration av förbund inom LO—planer, åtgärder och resultat," in *Organisationerna i det moderna samhället,* published by the State Council on Social Research (Uppsala: Almqvist & Wiksell, 1975), p. 80. Hadenius's article has been revised and incorporated in his doctoral thesis referred to earlier.

6. Rudolf Meidner and Berndt Öhman, *Solidarisk lönepolitik. Erfarenheter, problem, utsikter* (Stockholm: Tiden, 1972), pp. 9–10.

7. Ibid.

8. Ibid.

9. Motion 224, Minutes of the LO Congress of 1936, pp. 447–450. Motion 144 of the LO Congress of 1922 is generally considered the embryo of the wage policy of solidarity. Local 1 of the Metal Workers' Union in Stockholm introduced Motion 144, which spoke of "priority for support of the lowest paid membership groups" (Minutes of the LO Congress, 1922, pp. 283–284).

10. *Fackföreningsrörelsen och näringslivet;* Minutes of the LO Congress, 1941. See also Albin Lind, *Solidarisk lönepolitik* [A Wage Policy of Solidarity] (Stockholm: Tiden, 1938), as an example of initiatives undertaken in the 1930s.

11. Their more important articles were published in the Social Democratic magazines *Tiden* (1948) and *Fackföreningsrörelsen* (1949).

12. *Fackföreningsrörelsen och den fulla sysselsättningen* [The Labor Union Movement and Full Employment] (Stockholm: Tiden, 1951).

13. On the ideology of the new labor market policy and its relation to political theory see Leif Lewin, *Planhushållningsdebatten* (Stockholm: Almqvist & Wiksell, 1967), pp. 367–374, 412–416, 423–447.

14. See, for example, ibid. p. 475.

15. A different and widely held opinion on cause and effect in this connection is often encountered in print. According to this view, which takes a more flattering view of LO's actions, it was not general economic considerations that prompted LO to adopt central negotiations, but egalitarian wage political objectives. See Nils Elvander, *Intresseorganisationerna i dagens Sverige* 2d rev. ed. (Lund: Gleerup, 1969). "The deciding factor in LO's decision to move to central negotiations as of 1956 was the wage policy of solidarity" (p. 114). Within this project this question has been taken up by Axel Hadenius in his previously mentioned dissertation; see especially pp. 116–121.

16. Rudolf Meidner, "Samordning och solidarisk lönepolitik under tre decennier," in *Tvärsnitt. Sju forskningsrapporter utgivna till LOs 75-årsjubileum* (Stockholm: Prisma och Landsorganisationen i Sverige, 1973), p. 54.

17. Meidner and Öhman, *Solidarisk Lönepolitik. Erfarenheter, problem, utsikter,* p. 43.

18. *Konstitutionsutskottets betänkande* [Parliamentary Records], no. 26

(1973), pp. 110–111. See also ibid. no. 54 (1974), pp. 3–4, and no. 56 (1975/1976), p. 86.

19. Program copy for election special *Aktuellt* (Swedish television news, Channel 1), 12 September 1973.

20. Sven F. Bengtson, *Vi eller dom. Om facklig demokrati* (Stockholm: Tiden, 1971), pp. 64–68.

21. Jan Lindhagen and Macke Nilsson, *Hotet mot arbetarrörelsen* (Stockholm: Tiden, 1970), pp. 19–21.

22. One of the foremost exceptions to this generalization is Albin Lind's pamphlet from the 1930s, *Solidarisk lönepolitik,* especially pp. 18–26. Lind reflects on the "psychologically and organizationally" (p. 18) determined development toward a wage policy of solidarity. In the early years of industrialism the workers' moral sense of solidarity was psychologically incapable of encompassing the entire labor market. In practice, class solidarity was confined to the immediate fellow workers. In order to broaden the sense of solidarity, it was necessary "for the individual to undergo an educational process which resulted in the replacement of the deeply rooted individualism by a collective way of life and collective action" (p. 19). Thus, it happened that "out of this locally oriented sense of solidarity grew a widening of the area of solidarity to include the trade . . . He who worked at a trade and through this gained firsthand knowledge of the problems of income, job, and rights had no difficulty understanding that his colleagues in other places were wrestling with the same or similar problems. This simple fact constituted the constructive element in the widening of the sense of solidarity from the local area to include the trade as a whole. The third step in this development was taken as experience from the bargaining process and insight into how changes in the economy affected the industrial situation grew. This resulted in the gradual orientation of union organization along industrial lines. Through the breakthrough of the principle of industrial unions the framework of union solidarity was widened to extend its main tenets beyond the personal ken of the individual" (p. 19).

The quotations from Lind are interesting in two ways. First, he attempts to analyze the concept of solidarity, even though he tries to pass his own arguments and value judgments off as history. Second, his analysis is consistent with an attempt at interpreting the wage policy of solidarity as public spirit, applied to a union situation. The notion of solidarity as a result of an educational process of the individual members through which their horizons are widened beyond their individual ken is reminiscent of John Stuart Mill's views.

23. Phenomena 30 and 32 through 37 constitute the independent variables of this study. Phenomenon 31—the attitude expressed by members and leadership toward the district branch reform—is only an incidental aspect of phenomenon 30, organizational structure.

24. This figure may also be used in order to differentiate further between the Rousseauist concept and the model of interactive democracy. In this model, economic equality is only one value that the independent variable "wages" may assume, a contributing factor to the level of democratic development in a given organization. The Rousseauists, on the other hand, place equality at the very center of their view of democracy; all other circumstances

are subordinated to this one objective and are arranged to achieve maximum equality.

3. Members and Leaders: Agreement and Disagreement

1. This section, somewhat technical, may be skimmed by readers not interested in methodological questions. The data and the details of the fieldwork are presented in greater detail in *Kodbok till fackföreningsundersökningen* [Code Book for the Trade Union Study], (Stockholm: Rabén & Sjögren, 1977).

2. A fifth level—journalists and opinion makers—was added, for which sampling and fieldwork was done along with the others. The results are accounted for in Leif Lewin, *Åsiktsjournalistiken och den fackliga demokratin* (Stockholm: Rabén & Sjögren, 1977).

3. Barbro Lewin has been mainly responsible for the preparation of the sample, the fieldwork, and the coding process. Assisting in the fieldwork were Birgitta Döme, Ingrid Lindström, and Ewa Tures, and in committing it to paper Gunilla Arfwedson, Rut Carlsson, Inger Christoffersson, Gun Johansson, Jan-Erik Pettersson, and Krister Westerlund. Dorrit Alopaeus-Ståhl translated the questionnaire into Finnish.

4. The main responsibility for the sample belongs to Bo Jansson. Assistant professor Tore Dalenius gave valuable advice.

5. The political party preferences of the membership are instead shown through sample analysis; see table 3.34.

6. In a large-scale empirical research project on the political mobilization of the Swedish electorate from the end of the nineteenth century to our time, multicollinearity proved the most difficult problem to resolve. Given the method used at the time, the so-called political aggregate analysis with geographical units as observations, the problem was largely beyond our control. Farmers and agricultural workers on the one hand, and employers and workers, on the other, live in the same areas. The high geographical correlation between these coupled social classes used as independent variables corresponds to reality. Survey analysis has proved a better method for lowering multicollinearity in this area by means of reclassification and establishing limits. See Leif Lewin, *The Swedish Electorate, 1887–1968* (Stockholm: Almqvist & Wiksell, 1972), pp. 117–118 and 121–125.

7. The account will be as brief as possible. The technical complications encountered during fieldwork, for example, letters returned by the post office, wrong addresses, correspondence with unwilling participants, and so forth, will not be discussed.

8. Responses are weighted when the following are discussed: (1) Social Democratic or Communist locals; (2) the size of the local; and (3) individuals included in the original sample or the nonrespondent sample.

9. Dag Sörbom was mainly responsible for the data processing.

10. Ever since Theodore Adorno et al., *The Authoritarian Personality* (New York: Harper & Brothers, 1950) and the ensuing methodological debate, social scientists have been aware of the difficulties brought about by the ability of the more highly educated interviewees to formulate a critical response (for

example, "do not agree" rather than "agree"). They are also more aware of what the expected response would be and, to a certain extent, adapt their answer accordingly. They might for instance prefer to express agreement with the official program of the trade union movement rather than register a divergent opinion. This has probably affected the findings in this study to some extent, but the difference between the various levels is so pronounced that the main picture emerging would in all probability remain unchanged.

11. These questions and many others have been inspired by earlier trade union studies, especially *En studie av medlemmar och organisation i Kommunalarbetareförbundet. Rapport 1* (mimeographed, Group for Social Research, Social Democratic Party, Stockholm 1973).

"Voting in union elections" is not indicated as a measure of activity, because in a comparison between the responses of the test inverviews and the actual voting figures the claim of voting participation was so exaggerated that the measure proved useless in a study of this magnitude. (Some locals claimed voting figures that proved to be more than twice as high as the actual voting participation!)

12. Our sample design does not allow a corresponding correlation of section committee members and the general membership.

13. For more details on membership opinion and the personal views of the committee members see the data presented in the Code Book.

14. This figure in table 3.20 could have been higher, since the majority of those respondents (23 out of 31) who indicated "unemployment support" as "other reasons" could easily have been grouped with the response alternative "I find it useful to belong."

15. Validity test of the measure of "legitimacy":

Democratic Values	Percentage of Total	Percentage of Noncritics
Meeting activity	39	46
Discussion of union issues	27	29
Study activity	11	16
Reading of periodical	28	20
Forego a raise	47	34
Support low-income earners	78	73
Union dissatisfaction	61	58

16. W. S. Robinson, "The Statistical Measurement of Agreement," *American Sociological Review,* 22 (1957), 17–25. More about Robinson's Index in the Code Book.

To political scientists Robinson is better known for "the ecological error"; see Lewin, *The Swedish Electorate 1887–1968,* pp. 14–16, 15 n., and 261.

17. Cf. *En studie av medlemmar och organisation i Kommunalarbetareförbundet. Rapport 1,* p. 2:21.

18. As in other questions, the central level was actually more radical (see table 3.37, question 2).

19. This view of democracy and authority has been influenced by Robert A. Dahl, *Authority in a Good Society* (New Haven: Yale University Press, 1970).

20. Amitai Etzioni, *The Active Society. A Theory of Societal and Political Processes* (New York: Free Press, 1968), pp. 357–358, 370–373; also pp. 96–98 and 300.

4. Variations in the Form of Trade Union Government

1. For a more technical and detailed description, see *Kodbok till fackföreningsundersökningen* (Stockholm: Rabén & Sjögren, 1977).

2. In the case of competence, the committee members at the section level were thus limited to a maximum of 6 points, while at the local level 10 points were possible. Because the summary measurement of the score was expressed as a percentage of the total possible score, the section leaders were not in any way "disadvantaged."

3. As mentioned in note 2 above, the summary measurement was expressed in points based on the percentage of possible points.

4. It would have been theoretically possible to arrive at five single-variable cases, because five variable values fell within the "uncertainty zone." But in order for the classification to be usable in an explanatory analysis more than one or two locals would have to fall within a certain category. The five theoretical single-variable cases include acceptable consensus alone (two cases), and acceptable authority alone (three cases). There are no locals in the samples that might even theoretically be interpreted as acceptable opinion-formation alone. The second rule of interpretation was applied, and the two locals whose value might possibly have been interpreted as agreement of opinion alone were placed in category (b). The three locals whose variable value might theoretically have been authority alone were placed in category (c). The other 45 locals did not qualify as single-variable cases.

5. Whenever someone asked what might be the expected practical implications of this project I tried to anticipate the correlation between organizational structure and form of government, and claimed that if passivity decreases at the transition from smaller to larger units but high values for democracy were only found in district branches with representational bodies, this could be interpreted as a practical recommendation to the decision-makers to adopt representation. This view now appears to be wrong. On the extent to which the therapeutic form of government is dependent on district branches with representational bodies see table 4.6.

6. The correlation between public spirit and form of government will be tested in the next section. Out of the six district branches with representational bodies which were included in the therapeutic square none assumed the value "high degree of public spirit," three assumed "medium," and three "low degree of public spirit."

7. To a Swedish academic the participatory committees of the various departments at the universities constitute a prime example of a therapeutic form of government. The different groups have been guaranteed influence by the State. Consequently groups lacking interest in or insight into the problems

of teaching or research have the right to participate in decisions in these areas and not only in those directly concerning their own employment or place of work. Consensus-building has been poor, as might be expected, and, apart from a few sensitive situations in the aftermath of the dying student revolt, the participation of students and technical and administrative personnel has become ineffective. It is thus a kind of "therapy," creating calm by maintaining an illusion of co-determination.

8.   High wages (N=15)

High public spirit	33%
Medium	47
Low	20
Total	100

Medium wages (N=19)

High public spirit	42
Medium	37
Low	21
Total	100

Low wages (N=16)

High public spirit	31
Medium	25
Low	44
Total	100

9.   High wages (N=15)

Few wildcat strikes	53%
Medium	33
Many	13
Total	99

Medium wages (N=19)

Few wildcat strikes	21
Medium	63
Many	16
Total	100

Low wages (N=16)

Few wildcat strikes	6
Medium	44
Many	50
Total	100

(For high wages, the sum is less than 100 percent because of rounding to whole numbers.)

10. The computer program used for three analyses—requisite conditions, predictive power, and summary measure of the effect—was developed by Frank M. Andrews and Robert C. Messenger, *Multivariate Nominal Scale Analysis. A Report on a New Analysis Technique and a Computer Program* (Survey Research Center, Institute for Social Research, The University of Michigan, Ann Arbor, Michigan, 1973). The program is referred to as MNA. My thanks to my research assistant Olof Petersson, who drew my attention to this program.

11. See Leif Lewin, *Statskunskapen, ideologierna och den politiska verkligheten* (Stockholm: Rabén & Sjögren, 1972), pp. 23–26.

12. There are many indications that the three middle forms—the impotent, manipulative, and therapeutic forms of government—are not normatively equivalent. Thus the impotent form appears the "best" and most closely related to the democratic form. These locals as a rule show very high values for opinion-formation and consensus; only the presence of wildcat strikes prevents them from being classed as democratic. Correspondingly, the therapeutic form is the "least desirable" and the most closely related to the passive form of government. These locals often have low values, not only for consensus, which they lack by definition, but also for opinion-formation. In addition to the relationship predicted by the computer, the distribution of decision-nondecision is important. In this area, the values of the impotent locals were equal to those of the democratic, the therapeutic locals were the least satisfactory of the three middle forms, and the manipulative locals were in between. The proximity of the democratic and the impotent forms of government is hinted at through the similarity of their requisite conditions. Certain classification figures also point to the same internal order among the three middle forms with the mobility variable for the immigrant locals concentrated in the therapeutic and passive forms of government where also, to a lesser extent, the rather poor and predominantly female locals are found. Thus, the five forms of government could be normatively ranked as follows: (1) democratic, (2) impotent, (3) manipulative, (4) therapeutic, and (5) passive.

13. Here is further indication of the proximity between the impotent and the democratic locals.

Index

Agreement of opinion, *see* Representativity
Allen, V. L., 9
American Typographical Union, 15
Apathy, 14, 48–52
Authoritative execution, 24, 27
Authority, 7–8, 27–28, 60, 108–110, 129, 158–159

Bachrach, P., 105–106
Baratz, M., 105–106
Bargaining, 32–33, 40; conferences, 34–35; councils, 35
Blau, Peter M., 8–9
Bohman, B. Gösta, 47
Bossism, 35–36, 88, 157, 162–163
Brunnsvik People's High School, 48
Bureaucracy, 6, 8–9

Capitalism, 10–11
Capitalism, Socialism, and Democracy (Schumpeter), 13
Careerism, 88–89, 90
Carleson, C. N., 6
Center Party, 87, 158
Centralism, 6, 9–10
Collective affiliation, *see* Social Democratic Party (Sweden)
Comintern, 12
Communist Party, 44–45, 46, 87, 142, 158
Competence, of union leaders, 24, 81–84
Competition, among elites, 13–15, 27, 92–95
Compulsion, 48, 85
Conformism, 48, 85, 164
Consensus, 15, 18, 19, 20, 26–27

Consensus-building, 57, 129; as function of democracy, 23–24, 25; in LO, 90–105, 156–158
Contrat social (Rousseau), 5–6

December Compromise, 30
Decision-nondecision, 24, 26–27, 28, 57, 60, 105–108
Demands, 26, 27, 28, 57, 101–104, 158
Democracy, 9–10, 14, 16–17, 19, 151–152; direct, 5–6, 20, 55, 152; competitive, 14–15, 55, 152; representative, 15, 17, 19, 21, 29–30, 55; in locals, 130, 139, 140–141, 144, 159–160. *See also* Interactive democracy
Dissatisfaction, *see* Demands
District branches, 33–35, 110–111, 132–135, 161

Education, 17, 21, 47–48, 52. *See also* Schooling
Elections, union, 37, 91–96
Electorate, 13, 14
Elites, *see* Leadership
Empirical theory, 4–5
Employment, full, 38
Engels, Friedrich, 11
Erlander, Tage, 26
Etzioni, Amitai, 110

Fackföreningsrörelsen [Trade Union Movement], 9–10
Fackliga centralorganisationerna [FCO, Local Trade Councils], 48
Fackliga Propagandaförbundet [Union Propaganda Association], 12–13
Fieldwork, 68–72